AT HOME IN THE WORLD

BIBLIOTHECA HIMALAYICA
SERIES IV
VOLUME 2

ECOLOGY – ENVIRONMENT – DEVELOPMENT

THE PURPOSE OF
BIBLIOTHECA HIMALAYICA
IS TO MAKE AVAILABLE WORKS
ON THE CIVILIZATIONS AND NATURAL
HISTORY OF CENTRAL ASIA AND THE HIMALAYA

At Home in the World
Globalization and the Peace Corps in Nepal

James F. Fisher

Orchid Press

James F. Fisher
AT HOME IN THE WORLD:
Globalization and the Peace Corps in Nepal

First edition, copyright © James F. Fisher 2013

ORCHID PRESS
P.O. Box 1046,
Silom Post Office,
Bangkok 10504, Thailand
www.orchidbooks.com

BIBLIOTHECA HIMALAYICA
Copyright © The Estate of H. K. Kuloy

Front cover image: Author Jim Fisher adds a brick to the wall of a latrine at the high school in Dhulikhel.

Back cover image: Using cardboard models, Rolf Goetze explains his architectural plans for a new college building in Pokhara to the School Board.

ISBN 978-974-524-157-2

For my beloved Ursula

TABLE OF CONTENTS

LIST OF ILLUSTRATIONS

Image Sources:

Photographs 1, 3, 4, 5, 6, 8, 9, 10, 11, 15, 17 and 19 – Paul Conklin.

Photograph 14 – Dan Pierce.

All other photographs including front and back cover images – Jim Fisher.

ACKNOWLEDGEMENTS

My foremost debt of gratitude belongs, of course, to the members of Nepal I (pronounced "Nepal One")—the bureaucratic label with which we were tagged by Peace Corps headquarters in Washington, and the way we still, with puckish and pioneering pride, refer to ourselves. I have been talking to the people of Nepal I off and on during most of the last 50 years. The bulk of these conversations took place in Nepal a long time ago, but after our return to this country they resumed, sporadically, in group newsletters and at four reunions: the 25th, 30th, 38th, and 44th. I especially appreciate the time and thoughtful responses of those who submitted themselves to my relentless interviewing in more recent years. Without them there would be no book.

On the more scholarly and editorial front, I thank Nancy Wilkie for giving an early version of the manuscript the benefit of her astute editorial eye; Van Dusenbery for educating me in the wide world of globalization scholarship, which he knows so thoroughly; a few of the "natives" who read the rough draft and added bits and pieces to it from their own experiences; Kim Fisher for spotting problem areas early on and recommending solutions; Tom Robertson, for his extraordinarily careful and constructive reading and myriad editorial, substantive, and theoretical suggestions, all of which helped make the book more readable to the general public; and finally, Maya Fisher, for her painstaking, meticulous, and thorough recasting of the rough drafts that preceded the final version of this book, as well as the version that emerged at the end; without her editorial expertise, the book would still be languishing, in disarray, somewhere in my computer files.

I also greatly appreciate the support of Carleton College, in the form of research assistance from student workers, particularly students from Nepal who helped transcribe interview texts and organize and summarize data. In this regard I would like to acknowledge in particular the assistance of Abhinab Basnyat, for his careful attention to computerized summaries of information gleaned from the interviews. I thank Carleton further for the sabbaticals and additional competitive leaves that provided released time from teaching since I began working, off and on, on this project.

I should add, finally, that in a very realistic, humbling, and more than metaphorical sense, it is 50 years since I started working on this book.

PREFACE

On September 24, 1962, a small group of Americans, most of them (including me) in their early twenties, walked down the steps of a two engine, propeller-driven DC-3 (the old workhorse plane from World War II, of which there are 400 still flying in various parts of the world) that had just landed at the tiny airport in Kathmandu, Nepal. It had brought them from the fusty atmosphere of Delhi, down on the plains of India, up into the fresh mountain breezes wafting down from the Himalayas towering above the city. The airport used to be called Gauchar ("cow pasture", which is what it was originally), but now it was known as Tribhuvan International Airport. Tribhuvan was the eighth King in the Shah dynasty, who, in 1950, escaped from his palace, which had become his prison, and overthrew the Ranas, the despotic family of hereditary Prime Ministers who had ruled Nepal for more than a century. Our trip had begun at Idlewild, which, like the Kathmandu airport, is also now named for a national hero (JFK), aboard a larger plane, this one with four propellers. The Americans were the first Peace Corps Volunteers to arrive in Nepal. Wanting to make a good first impression, they were, by the standards of the day, dressed up—some of the men wore ties, apparel they would not don again while in Nepal.

They were carrying backpacks filled with whatever they thought they might need at first in this new land. Like many other circumstances they encountered, what to bring with them was a matter of conjecture; since they were the first Volunteers to Nepal, they had nothing to go on other than what they had learned during three months of training in the U.S., and who could say how reliable that information was? In their heads they were carrying something else: a wide-ranging mixture of hopes and fears, reflecting the excitement and nervousness they felt about how all this was going to go. Training is one thing, but being on the ground in Nepal was the real thing. They were to spend two years in Nepal working in education and agriculture and learning about Nepalese life by eating the food and speaking the language of the Nepalis who, they fervently hoped, would become their friends, neighbors, and co-workers. Although neither the Volunteers nor anyone else knew it at the time, they were also part of something bigger than they were, something that would later come to be called, without a great deal of semantic precision, a worldwide process of "globalization."

Nepal is often described, a little inaccurately and unfairly, as miniature, simply because, compared to its two colossal neighbors, India and China, it does indeed seem very small. But dozens of other countries in the world are even smaller—e.g., Greece, Korea, Cuba—but they are not particularly thought of in that diminutive way because they are not located next door to giants. Nepal is roughly the size and shape of Tennessee, but its population of more than 30 million (in 2012) is about the same as California's, inhabiting an area roughly three times that of Nepal.

Although roiling in politics (Tribhuvan's son, Mahendra, had jailed the country's first elected Prime Minister a little over a year before our arrival) Nepal in 1962 seemed quiet and undisturbed by the buzz of the outside world. The capital city, Kathmandu, had few cars on its streets, and its temple architecture, highly wrought from stone and delicately carved wood, was still suffused with a medieval ambiance. A road south to India had been completed only about five years before, and a road north to Tibet had not gotten past the talking stage. The American government was pressuring Nepal not to allow the Chinese to build such a road. King Mahendra told the Americans communism would not come to Nepal in a taxi, and within a few years the road was built. Very few goods came down that road from Tibet to Nepal, and communism was not among them.

The main mode of transportation outside of the Kathmandu Valley was by foot, on mountain trails; goods such as cloth, cigarettes, tennis shoes, and food were carried on the human back. It would have taken two or three months to traverse the 500 mile country, assuming anyone was inclined to do so. The easier route would have been to cross the border into India, travel on its buses and trains, and then cross back into Nepal at the other end.

Some 10 million people, in 1962, lived in the mountains and in the plains bordering India, the overwhelming majority of them farmers. Villages ranged in size from the odd homestead or two to hundreds of houses. Houses were made from stone, wood, and bamboo, or all of the above, stuccoed with mud, depending on what materials were available. Daily life followed the seasons and their plowing, planting, and harvesting cycles, and the movement of animals, such as taking yak to high pastures in summer and down again in winter. People came to urban centers like Kathmandu rarely or not at all, whether to buy things in the markets or to make pilgrimages to the many temples and shrines there. Schools were rare, except in a few small towns, as were hospitals.

In this pre-tourist age, when Peace Corps Volunteers walked into villages, especially remote ones, we were sometimes the first European people villagers had seen. Each was equally puzzled by the other. The most common village reaction was simply to stare at the white strangers, as if they couldn't quite believe what they were seeing and were wondering what kind of animal we were. Sometimes they would rub my arm to see if the white color was real, or if, somehow just painted on, it would rub off. Our reaction was to try out our rudimentary Nepali, which was usually at least good for a laugh. The fact that we clearly didn't speak the language well was trumped by their surprise that we spoke it at all. In those days almost none of the few foreigners living in Nepal (diplomats, USAID workers, a handful of missionaries; tourists were almost nonexistent) spoke any Nepali.

It is tempting to think of rural villages as quiet, peaceful, idyllic places, but they were often noisy—roosters announcing the dawn even when it was still dark, dogs barking, people yelling from one house to another, sometimes socially, perhaps to arrange a day of cooperative work in the fields, sometimes arguing about some real or imagined slight. The rhythm of daily life was often punctuated by this or that festival, whether religious or simply marking the passing of seasons or life cycles including, but not limited to, births, marriages, and deaths. For Peace Corps Volunteers coming from relatively fast-paced mechanized urban or rural lives it was a world about which we had little intuitive understanding. Our training staff had presented us with ample facts and figures about Nepal, but not how to comprehend this swirl of humanity. What were they doing? What were they thinking? What were they saying? These were all questions that dumbfounded us at first, and to some extent continued to puzzle us over the two years we spent in the country.

It would be well to begin by stating what this book is not. It is not primarily about globalization, using the experiences of these Volunteers as convenient examples. It's more the other way around. First and foremost it is the story of the Volunteers themselves. It attempts to tell, largely in their own voices, how their lives, and the lives of those they touched, in Nepal and later in the U.S., were transformed and informed by the on-going globalization of which they were inexorably, if unwittingly, a part.

The subject of this book is also not the history of the Peace Corps, about which a number of books have been written. It is not even a history of the Peace Corps in Nepal. Instead, it consists mostly of the stories and the histories of a few real, named people living in real time in real space with real Nepalis. It asks why these Volunteers applied to the Peace Corps in the first place, how they were trained, what they wanted to do in Nepal and what they did there (not always the same thing), and what happened to them, and to Nepal and to America, in the 50 years since their arrival that halcyon September day.

The book also makes no claim to being an in-depth analysis of our effect on Nepal, although it makes periodic, anecdotal forays in that direction, since of course without the Nepalis we came to know, none of what we did, thought, and learned would have happened. Most of our Nepalese friends had long since scattered we knew not where, so I could talk to very few of them, particularly those I knew only through the intermediaries of Volunteers who had known them. Its emphasis is therefore on the Americans, partly because they comprise a convenient universe, but also because, globalization notwithstanding, I still identify strongly with my Peace Corps mates. I understand them better because I know them better. We're native speakers of the same language.

At its inception and at its heart, although its content centers on the Nepal I group as a whole, this book ultimately stems from my desire to understand my own experience and life. But although this is less a rigorous academic exercise than a look at my personal experience, I am no memoirist; I am an anthropologist, and my way of understanding is to look at my subjects through an anthropological lens. Here I look at them—or, I should say, us—in a special way: as people who were, and are, part of a continuing process of globalization.

By now it will be no surprise that this book is not the sort of compendium or summary of what has happened to, for example, the graduates of a high school or college fifty years after commencement. The present effort bears no resemblance to such albums, with their thumbnail paragraph or one-page sketches of the lives of each graduate. One unintended result of the approach I have chosen is that many of my fellow Volunteers are not individually mentioned, although they are all caught in the statistical net employed sometimes. Instead, I have elected to quote, often at considerable length, only those whose stories were most compelling or instructive, in the belief that their narratives distill and clarify experiences shared in varying but often less elucidating ways by the rest of us, the silent majority who are not so cited.

Fig. 1. Peace Corps Director Sargent Shriver on a visit to Volunteers in Nepal, January 1964; the face peering over his left shoulder is that of the author. (See also Appendix II for further details of this visit.)

1

INTRODUCTION: AMBIGUOUS IMPERIALISTS?

"Ask not what your country can do for you—ask what you can do for your country." is the way John F. Kennedy put it in that ringing phrase at the end of his inaugural Presidential address in 1961. He had been no less hortatory earlier in his speech, when he said that every nation should know, "whether it wishes us well or ill, that we shall pay any price, bear any burden, meet any hardship, support any friend, oppose any foe, in order to assure the survival and the success of liberty." The strength and spirit that lay behind all these verbal pyrotechnics were eventually summed up, during the short duration of his Presidency, under the moniker of "The New Frontier."

The vigorous, vibrant New Frontier of the new decade of the 1960s was seen and promoted as the antithesis of the listless, dispirited, even boring 1950s business-dominated society with its grey flannel suits, Levittown housing, and an elderly General in the White House. The 1950s were regarded by New Frontiersmen as an age of relaxed, complacent people comfortable and satisfied with their way of life and blandly optimistic about the future.[1] By the dawn of the 1960s, the younger cohorts of the population found it all a little hollow; they were ready to dive into something different, challenging, even daring.

Kennedy's was high oratory, indeed, but in practice there were not that many ways to go about responding to his plea, assuming one were moved by it to do so. One of the first ways Kennedy responded to his own challenge was the issuance of an executive order, less than two months after taking office, aimed at initiating a novel kind of government agency which, after some initial terminological uncertainty, came to be called the Peace Corps.[*]

In the Peace Corps Act that was soon passed by Congress (Kennedy signed it into law September 22, 1961), the Peace Corps was mandated to provide trained manpower to developing countries and increase understanding of America in these countries and vice versa, which was, in its own nationalistic way, globalization without the term. Such an initiative was greeted with skepticism in many quarters, including those of conservative Republicans who dismissed it by nicknaming it the "Kiddie Corps." Richard Nixon said it would be a haven for draft-dodgers, although service in the Peace Corps did not satisfy the requirement of military service then in effect. Mere mocking did not defeat it, however, because it was an idea whose time had come, an image much like the "shining city on a hill" that Ronald Reagan later used to sum up the notion of American Exceptionalism. In the subsequent rhetoric of the times, the Americans who enlisted in the Peace Corps were often characterized (sometimes but not always accurately, as the narratives below will demonstrate) as "answering Kennedy's call."[†]

This book attempts to draw a portrait of how the Peace Corps, as a partial personification of Kennedy's idealism, rooted in notions of evangelical outreach going back to the founding of the republic, worked out. It does so not by drawing an encyclopedic portrait of the Peace Corps in general, but by describing a very specific case: that of the first group of Volunteers to Nepal, one of the first countries

---

[*]   In Nepali, "Peace Corps" translates roughly as "Peace Army" ("Shanti Sena"), reflecting the historical and ironic binary of Corps—Army and Peace—and the beautiful paradox that it evokes and expresses. The irony continues in Nepali as "Shanti Sena" is also used to refer to blue-helmeted U.N. Peacekeepers (including more than 5,000 Nepalis—another form of globalization) deployed throughout the world. Less auspiciously, Nepali pronunciations of the English "Peace Corps" sometimes came out as "Peace Corpse."

[†]   Although Kennedy established the Peace Corps, the idea had been kicking around since at least the 1950s. Hubert Humphrey introduced a Peace Corps bill in 1957; its reception in Congress was lukewarm.

to host Peace Corps Volunteers—how they were recruited and trained, what they did there, and what they've done during the 50 years since then. Since I was one of those Volunteers, this book is part documentary, part memoir, part confession. At their core, the interests that have resulted in this book began to develop, inchoate as they were, when I went to Nepal as a member of that first Peace Corps group; they have continued during my career as an anthropologist ever since then.

Like most of us in our group, I was captivated by Nepal from the get-go. I was immediately and utterly fascinated and bewildered by its various tribes, castes, languages, religions, rituals, cuisines, kinship types, family structures, economic life, music, and so forth—all the much described, and sometimes belabored, cultural diversity for which Nepal is justly famous.

Nepal is nothing if not diverse: in altitude, from 300 feet above sea level (along the southern border with India) to 29,035 feet above sea level (the summit of Mt. Everest, on the northern, Tibetan border), and in just about everything else—geology, flora, fauna, and, especially, culture, however it is defined. About 100 different languages are spoken in Nepal, whether by people of Tibeto-Burman origin, like the Sherpas, or by those of Indo-Aryan origin, like caste Hindus. Its people practice a variety of religions, mostly Hinduism and Buddhism, but, here and there, also Islam, Christianity, shamanism, various forms of animism, and even the occasional Baha'i.

In addition to Nepal's diversity, I was also intrigued by the juxtaposition of young and (I eventually concluded) naïve Americans next to people who had learned the lessons of life from their hardscrabble existence cultivating fields carved into steep terraces, herding animals on high pastures, and tending rice in verdant valleys. What could I possibly teach them, I wondered? A little, perhaps, but I wound up learning far more than whatever small amount of instruction I had to offer as an English teacher in the classroom.

Indeed, it is no hyperbole to say that the Peace Corps experience fundamentally transformed my life: that initial two-year commitment eventually grew into a lifetime of trying, as an anthropologist, to understand social and cultural change in Nepal as it has developed over the intervening years. To further that interest I have made research forays into remote areas of northwest Nepal (the Kaike-speaking Magars of Dolpa) and northeast Nepal (the Sherpas of Solu-Khumbu), as well as the high Hindu castes in Kathmandu[2] and other more central, urban areas. But in this book I go back to where, for me, it all began. I examine how I, and others in the group I was part of, experienced Nepal, and how we did so as part of what is commonly and casually referred to as the globalization of American and, necessarily, Nepalese society.

Those whose sentiments I found most quotable are by no means necessarily the "best" Volunteers; they simply represent the luck of the draw in my attempts to find and talk to people. I hope those who remain silent in these pages will find their thoughts and actions adequately represented by those of their comrades who are given voice here, as I have tried to mine the meaning and significance our experiences had for all of us. In that veiled and roundabout, but faithful, sense, this book is indeed about all of us who were a part of Nepal I.

Globalization

I have mentioned the globalization of American and Nepalese societies, but what does this term, "globalization," mean? The word was first coined as recently as 1950, a year when most of us in Nepal I were still in elementary or secondary school, and it was first used, or at least first popularized, in a scholarly way in a 1983 article in the *Harvard Business Review*.[3] By now it has achieved such common currency that one can hardly avoid it in newspapers, magazines, TV programs, or Internet blogs. It is a widely shared word which sounds as if its meaning should be transparent and unproblematic, but which, perversely, becomes harder to pin down the more closely one examines it.

What does it ultimately amount to? At its conceptual root it might be defined as the expansion and intensification of social relations and consciousness across time and space.[4] More briefly still, it may be thought of as a long-term but accelerating historical process of growing worldwide interconnectedness, the process of integrating nations and peoples into a larger community.[5] Definitions notwithstanding, unlike other "-ization" words, such as industrialization, urbanization, westernization, and modernization—all of them terms that seduced the post-World War II world (and which "globalization" is largely displacing)—globalization remains a vague and elusive concept.

What the term needs to flesh out its substance is not more bloodless abstractions, or an exegesis of "world-systems theory,"[6] but real-life examples capable of breathing shape, color, and sound into it.[7] This is easier said than done, however, because although the effects of globalization are powerful, the people doing the globalizing, or being globalized, are, as in the case of members of a culture, not necessarily aware of these forces. None of us who stuffed backpacks full of clothes and hopped on a Pan Am flight for Nepal in 1962 realized that we were the cutting edge of a process that would define a generation. For the most part we were clueless about all this.

Nevertheless, that is what I attempt to do in this book—to shrink globalization to a human level by looking closely at a small group of people (including myself), previously unknown to each other, who, in the midst of their everyday lives in the world of Elvis Presley and Fats Domino (the Beatles had not yet made it to the U.S.), and of Mickey Mantle and Cassius Clay (before he became Muhammad Ali), were caught up in the sudden onset of the worldwide globalizing pulse. Americans, some of whom had barely been off the farms they grew up on, or had never flown in an airplane, suddenly dropped out of the sky into Nepal. Even the more cosmopolitan among them had never been anywhere remotely resembling Nepal. Whatever effects we had or did not have *on* Nepal, during our two years *in* Nepal we encountered conditions which were utterly and entirely novel to us along a variety of dimensions: religious (Hindu and Buddhist), social (joint family), political (absolute monarchy), educational (rote memory), and dietary (*dal-bhat*, or rice and lentils). These dimensions of existence globalized us profoundly, although we didn't think of it that way. My aim, then, is to focus closely on these intimate human experiences of globalization, and my hope is that working on a smaller canvas in this way results in a picture featuring more vivid contrasts and sharper detail. The theory of globalization that results then arises from trying to interpret the picture, rather than prescribing how the picture should be drawn.

Of course, broadly understood, globalization is not a recent process at all. It has been underway for a very long time—as long as populations have been moving from place to place, whether across a river, an ocean, or a continent, packing ideas and ideologies along with the goods they bring with them. Certainly one might argue, in the American and Nepalese cases, that globalization has been a fundamental part of their national histories, with the unending, successive waves of immigrants from all over the world, beginning hundreds and even thousands of years ago. One hundred percent of the residents of Nepal and the U.S. are either immigrants or descendants of immigrants. The only question to debate is when the ancestors arrived.

Not only is globalization old as a demographic phenomenon, but even the idea of globalization is ancient, as seen in the reply Diogenese Laertius, the third-century historian of philosophy, made when anyone asked where he came from: his answer was always, "I am a citizen of the world". However, in this book I focus only on a recent stage in the growth of that globalization, one that dramatically altered its pace, scope, depth, and character as the last half of the 20th century came to a close. I do so in a very limited and small-scale way, yet the tidal forces of history are moved by powers that at first may seem small and distant.

Specifically, then, I examine globalization as it has been illustrated and played out among the members of the first group of American Peace Corps Volunteers to Nepal. Thus I concentrate on how one small piece fits into the larger and historical globalizing puzzle rather than dwell on the abstractions with which the notion of globalization is constructed. There are already enough polemics and profundities surrounding these ideas in the world, and not enough grounding of these ideas in the realities of how people live their everyday lives—waking up with a cup of morning tea, managing all the social and cultural obligations of their work-a-day world, and then falling asleep at night on a cotton-covered thin mat on the floor.

Scholarly definitions aside, as a vernacular buzzword the term globalization—ironically for a neologism—means different things to different people. It is part corporate hype and capitalist regulatory agenda,[8] part cultural excitement, part social commentary and protest. To the general American public, globalization is most often thought of as the beleaguering force behind such painful and ugly developments as out-sourcing, out-of-control immigration, and worldwide upheavals of banks and international financial markets.

This is one of the problems with thinking about globalization: the assumption that it is mostly about economics. Indeed, economists have successfully hijacked the term, as they often do—it is an ill wind that blows no economist good. What needs to be emphasized instead is that globalization involves issues other than the transaction of four trillion dollars worth of currencies every day, because globalization is also a human phenomenon— as illustrated by the fact that at any given time 500,000 people are sitting on airplanes. That is an economic fact of undoubted importance to the airline industry, but it is also important to those who are flying to new places and meeting new people, which will cause them to see the world, and their place in it, in new ways.

So, in addition to being economic, globalization is social, cultural, and demographic. But it is also experienced by individuals, grappling with it one by one. I therefore follow along the lines of social theorist Anthony Giddens' idea that "Globalization is not only about what is 'out there,' remote and far away from the individual. It is an 'in here' phenomenon too, influencing intimate and personal aspects of our lives."[9] Globalization usually conjures up huge, world-wide forces at play, but if globalization as a "taken-for-granted macro context and as an abstract process too big for ethnographic endeavor" can be challenged by investigating Wall Street investment bankers ethnographically, as has been done,[10] then Peace Corps Volunteers and their Nepalese friends and co-workers can certainly also serve as grist for the globalization mill.

The core phenomena I explore are the seismic changes American society began to experience about a half century ago in politics, gender, race, and profession, aided and abetted by a new wave of unprecedented voluntary peace activism. This study details how the identities of individual Volunteers were challenged, forged, and altered by their experiences with Nepalese society. It describes what has happened to them, to Nepal, to the United States, and to the world since then.

Using my anthropological training and background, I show how these developments have been part of a transformation of American society and Nepalese society, and how each has affected the other. Globalization is not simply a westernizing affair, nor can it be viewed solely as a homogenizing one. It is not just about the McDonaldization of the world.[11] It must be read instead as a complex process that brings the West to the rest and the rest to the West.[12] Through individual cameos, developed through the crucial crucible of two years in Nepal, I assemble portraits of U.S. society, and to some extent Nepalese society, then and now. America has also been reshaped by global forces, prominent among them Asian ones, such as food (Thai, Indian, Chinese), religion (various Indian gurus), music (especially Indian), demographics (perhaps a dozen or so Nepalese residents in the U.S. in 1962 vs. 60,000 in 2010).

My argument rests on the assumption that Peace Corps Volunteers can be seen as data points in the continuing paradigmatic shift that altered the U.S. and Nepal during these

50 years. One might object at this point that 70 Volunteers in a country of 10 million (the population of Nepal when we were there) could not make any impact worth mentioning. But in fact over a period of two years each Volunteer interacted with hundreds of Nepalis, and our relations, some of which were conducted in our fractured Nepali, were often personal and of some depth. The kind of relationships Volunteers experienced worldwide varied from country to country and the Peace Corps leadership in each. Fortunately, we shared precious little with our comrades in Latin America, where the Peace Corps encouraged Volunteers to regard the peasant farmer not as a human being but as "a useful receptacle for material and technical inputs."[13]

But to return to numbers: If 70 seems small, what about 3,629, which is the number of Peace Corps Volunteers who had served in Nepal by 2004, the year Peace Corps withdrew because living conditions had become too dangerous during the Maoist insurgency?* Or what of the many more thousands of Volunteers from other nations, such as Japan, UK, Germany, or Denmark, who followed us to Nepal? Or 200,000, which is the number of Peace Corps Volunteers who have served in some 139 countries over the last 50 years? Furthermore, many of these Volunteers became involved in life-long expat work; because they started so young, their impact lasted a very long time.

Anthropology and the Peace Corps

Traditionally, the more distant, inaccessible, obscure, and, especially, culturally different the societies anthropologists study are, the better. Famous examples include Margaret Mead's Samoans and Malinowski's Trobrianders, both Pacific Ocean island societies, and Evans-Pritchards' Nuer, cattle-herders in north Africa. However, anthropologists have not hesitated to "familiarize the exotic" by also studying large, complex, non-western but geopolitically important societies such as Japan or Turkey. In recent years they have

---

* The Peace Corps returned to Nepal in 2012.

increasingly turned their attention towards the last frontier: exoticizing (showing how even the most routine parts of our lives can be seen as strange by those who don't share them) the culture of familiar, mainstream, contemporary, middle-class America. Remaining true to their calling, however, they have gone about that in an anthropological fashion, by drawing on original and intensive fieldwork in small communities (even when they are located in large urban areas) rather than depending on data derived from government statistics, industrial reports, census figures, and survey research data sets.

I locate this book within all these traditions by combining, within a unified dialectical frame, the anthropology of a small South Asian country—Nepal—with that of a large, modern one—the United States of America. Rather than seeking to demonstrate how different and distinct each place is (the tried and true anthropological *modus operandi*, involving explicit or implicit comparison and contrast between discrete places, as Mead, Malinowski, and Evans-Prichard did), I try to show, in the face of exponentially increasing globalization, not just how neither can any longer be adequately understood without reference to the other, but how their social worlds are interconnected and how their fates have become inextricably intertwined.

Thus I not only build on both these traditions, but I try also to transcend them by incorporating the encompassing forces of globalization to create a third approach. This line of attack is critical of the notion of cultures as distinct, separate, and autonomous entities[14] (which is largely the way Mead, Malinowski, and Evans-Pritchard looked at it), rather than amalgams of meaning with highly fluid, permeable and unstable borders. I join Arjun Appadurai in thinking of cultural forms in today's world as "fundamentally fractal," that is, as possessing none of the boundaries, structures, or regularities anthropologists have traditionally ascribed to them. These globalizing and globalized "cultures" are characterized by disjunctive change, what Appadurai calls ebbs and flows[15] in a variety of elements that he describes with the following novel vocabulary: ethnoscapes, which have to do with people, ethnicities, immigrants, tourists, and the like; technoscapes, involving high and low technology, including mechanical and informational devices; financescapes, such as the spread and use of global capital; mediascapes, concerned with electronic, digital, TV, internet, and cinematic processes; and ideoscapes, referring to political and religious ideologies. Believing that ethnoscapes have been neglected compared to these other "scapes", I track the flows of ethnoscapes to the relative, but not total, exclusion of the other "scapes" that constitute Appadurai's globalizing world.

Context is crucial to this study ("context-driven" is the argot here), as it examines the dense connections in these various "scapes" between Asia and the U.S. by looking intensively at one of the smaller, seemingly marginal countries of the world. I argue not just that understanding one's own culture is enhanced by the view from another—one of the classic rationales for the existence of anthropology—but that the view from tertiary, peripheral regions enables one to see more clearly the primary, central ones.[16] I knew no better way to make this point to the anthropology students in my introductory class than to quote T. S. Eliot:

We shall not cease from exploration
And the end of all our exploring
Will be to arrive where we started
And know the place for the first time.[17]

Peace Corps: Who Benefits?

The Peace Corps was and is incontestably part of this accelerating, globalizing wave washing over the world; the Peace Corps was also ambiguous in character from the beginning. On the one hand, it continued the altruistic, sometimes soteriological-oriented, outward-looking ideology of social service that had informed American society from its very beginnings as the Puritans' "city on a hill."[18] On the other hand, the Peace Corps simultaneously generated and

nurtured international expertise increasingly needed by the
political and economic establishment. Later in the 1960s and
1970s, as the U.S. began to sink deeper into adventuristic
wars in Southeast Asia, the Peace Corps was critiqued as
complicit in them, providing benign cover for aggressive
military policies, as wolves in sheep's clothing. As reluctant
imperialists, America lacked the centuries of international
experience that the dominant, towering colonial powers
like Great Britain and France possessed. Internationally, or
globally, the United States has always been playing catch-up,
to satisfy its imperial ambitions to make the 20th Century what
Henry Luce called "The American Century". Was the Peace
Corps part of this late-in-the-game effort?

I approach the question of who benefits from the Peace
Corps by ethnographically cross-examining the three
purposes of the Peace Corps as defined by the Congressional
Act that created it in 1961: 1) providing trained manpower
to developing countries, 2) increasing understanding of
America in other countries, and 3) increasing understanding
of other countries in America. To begin with, this 1961
Congressional language is couched in the cant of countries
and internationalization, whereas I attempt to reframe these
issues in terms of culture and globalization.

Each of these three purposes, and all of them considered
together, raise an overarching and frequently debated
question: Did the Peace Corps represent seed money to
promote larger American interests in other countries as
part of an on-going imperialist project (perhaps even
an "orientalist" [19] one), by opening American doors,
introducing desires for American goods, and training a
generation of experts otherwise unavailable to American
corporations and the State Department? [20] President
Kennedy himself said as much to us at a reception on the
south lawn of the White House, on August 9, 1962: "We
are so in need of dedicated men and women of talent and
experience, that I can think of no more significant recruiting
ground than the Peace Corps for our future Foreign Service
Officers, for those who represent our information services
and aid agencies abroad."

Or, alternatively, is the conventional understanding of the Peace Corps more correct? This view holds that ulterior imperial motives, such as staffing government bureaucracies and multinational corporations, were not involved. This understanding holds that the Peace Corps is nothing more nor less than what it claims to be: an honest and benign experiment in 1) raising living standards in the poorer countries of Africa, Asia, and Latin America, and 2) raising international consciousness and understanding, here and in those so-called Third World countries.

As these interpretations are not inherently at cross-purposes, it is not only possible but also plausible that both are simultaneously true, which perhaps explains why they stubbornly continue to be debated.

Most discussions of this issue address it, ardently and single-mindedly, with this or that political axe to grind. Rather than attempting to resolve the question at that ideological level, I prefer instead to search for at least the beginnings of an answer in the fine-grained details of the character and activities of a small group on the ground in Nepali towns and villages in the early 1960s, and their fate over subsequent decades.

The answer to what the Peace Corps is, ontologically, needs to take account of what those who were in it did, and how they may have been used. There is a difference between Washington's short-term intentions, and on the ground realities and long-term consequences. To attend to the latter, it is not enough to understand what Volunteers were doing; we also need to grasp what they *thought* they were doing. This book constitutes an attempt to answer both questions.

Peace Corps, Nepal, and the U.S.

In line with the relatively recent anthropological interest in American society[21] (in contrast to the exotic interests of Mead, Malinowski, and Evans-Pritchard), this study is a retrospective look at what has happened since the first group of 70 American Peace Corps Volunteers went to Nepal. The Nepal experience provides a dynamic frame of reference for how specific individuals, whose lives were profoundly recast by their time in Nepal, ultimately contributed, in their own small way, to the transformation of the larger society in which they were rooted and nurtured. I ask what has happened over time: how the subsequent lives of those in this group were sharply altered—in class, education, and occupation—by this experience. I conclude by showing how these lives became a vital part of the increasingly globalized milieu of American society.

To acquire this evidentiary base I traveled extensively (and telephoned and, after the arrival of the internet, emailed those I couldn't reach otherwise) to record interviews with the far-flung members of this racially, ethnically, religiously, educationally, and economically diverse group. They have settled all over the world, so this study took place not only in two countries very distant from each other, but even within the U.S. my "informants" were scattered in different directions and settled in many different sites. The scatter-shot methodology required to gather information from all over the map for this project was required in order to address the multi-sitedness necessary[22] to stitch together an integrated portrait of people as diverse as we are.

The returned Nepal I Volunteers have held a cross-section of jobs that run the gamut of modern American occupations: teacher, farmer, government bureaucrat, banker, social worker, homemaker, mechanic, architect, international development professional, hotelier, educational administrator, real estate agent, writer, and lawyer, among others. Most of these occupational choices evolved directly or indirectly out of the Peace Corps experience. Without it, the 70 biographies that developed over the last five decades would for the most part have been those of unrecognizable strangers to themselves and to each other. For almost all, especially the great majority who were of college and immediate post-college age, those two years spent living and working in Nepal were a sharply defining, once-in-a-lifetime moment.

The heart of the project is contained in the wide-ranging, self-reflective narratives, reproduced Studs Terkel-style, which the interviews generated. They demonstrate the dramatic shifts in education, career choice, and life-chances that have marked the lives of almost everyone, while noting a general constancy of political and religious orientation. These narratives detail the psychological trajectories revealed by tracing back and forth internationally (or between cultures, as I would put it more anthropologically) since the Nepal years, and how those paths have played out in various domestic and international movements involving social and political issues such as civil rights, feminism, international development, war, and the environment.

The changes and transformations in individual lives which I describe as facts are more like intersecting hypotheses about the causes and effects of globalization that need to be tested—whether, for example, the Peace Corps is merely part of a new kind of colonialism.[23] The "proof" of such hypotheses would require control groups of people who had not gone to Nepal, speculations about what would have happened to Nepal without the Peace Corps, to the Peace Corps without Nepal, or to America without either— in other words, what the world would be like if it were different from what, in sheer actuality, it is.

Those are not my projects, although others might undertake them, perhaps using this study as supportive or contradicting data. But what about the other half of the story: the changes in Nepal and the Nepalis we worked with and got to know? Ideally, I would chart not only the changes in American lives, but, to the extent that it is possible, also trace the effects of the Volunteers' residence and work *in* Nepal *on* Nepal and Nepalis,* including their views of the Peace Corps Volunteers that they got, in random fashion, to know. Though the clues have grown cold over the years, I do so when and where the information is available, from

---

*　I did a version of this in *Sherpas* (Berkeley: University of California Press, 1990), in which I trace the effects on Nepal of building the airstrip at Lukla and several village schools.

the Volunteers who kept up, since the dialectic cannot be avoided.

This book sheds light on such big and broad questions as *how* and *why* globalization has become such a powerful contemporary force in the world. It will also be a follow-up study, not of the kind in which anthropologists return to their villages, but of the diaspora of individuals who once formed an intense and intentional, if dispersed and dislocated, community. The main difference between this "village" of Peace Corps Volunteers and a traditional anthropological village is that the natives of the Peace Corps Village grew up separately and now live, mostly, in separate locations— many on opposite sides of the country, some on opposite sides of the globe. But they nonetheless remain an "imagined community"[24] in the most committed and impassioned sense of that term.

What this book describes is also noteworthy because, surprisingly, no such ethnography of Peace Corps Volunteers exists. Various reports and reviews of the Peace Corps have of course appeared over the years.[25] But these tend to scrutinize one Volunteer's idiosyncratic experience, or analyze how the bureaucracy works, rather than how incipient components of globalization begin to form and take shape. Such studies are not ethnographically and theoretically grounded in the manner of the one I propose here.

Uprooted both abruptly and voluntarily (they were, after all, volunteers), they had grown up before the world came to America in living color on live television. They were on the cusp of revolutionary changes brought about by satellite communications, computers, and cheap jet travel. The number of trans-Atlantic telephone conversations soared from 250,000 in 1957 to 4.3 million in 1961.[26] Such numbers moved Marshall McLuhan to proclaim the world a "global village" in 1962, the year live television was first transmitted across the Atlantic and the year the first Volunteers headed for Nepal.

Thus the Peace Corps, representing the cultural component of globalization, was the entering wedge of non-military, non-corporate, non-religious American internationalism. As a narrative of what might be called establishment peace activism during the Cold War, as a critique of the dominant culture of the time (the culture of the 1950s, which we were trying to transcend or transform), and as an illustration and early instance of novel transnational flows[27] (essential elements of globalization) which have now become quotidian, the book covers very significant historical ground.

The history of the second half of the 20th century will be dry as dust without the views of those who lived through and embodied it, especially those who were present at the creation of such a quantum shift in American and international life. This was, after all, a time when post-World War II American hegemony abroad was beginning to be challenged, and when wide-spread domestic discontent over civil rights was just getting underway. The macro-phenomena that command contemporary headlines—globalization, transnationalism, orientalism, migration, internationalization—cannot be adequately understood without the micro agents who instantiate them.

The creation of the Peace Corps demonstrates that the early '60s were not times of business as usual. They were just the opposite: times of business as *un*usual. We live in their wash, whatever conservative and liberal turns the U.S. has taken, or the Maoist insurgency—now the most powerful political and legal entity in Nepal—has undergone, since then. The ironic relation of the Peace Corps to these subsequent unintended consequences forms part of the interview discussions.

Insider vs. Outsider

This is as good a point as any to acknowledge specifically that, as a member of this group myself, I lay claim not only to familiarity with objective, quantifiable facts available to anyone with the interest to pursue them, but also to knowledge of the subjective and intuitive components that underlay the experiences we shared. Far from being

a disembodied and unengaged objective spectator, I have
been ageing and changing along with other Volunteers and
Nepalis—we all wear the same watches. My anthropology
career developed on foundations constructed by issues
encountered during Peace Corps times, but the person who
encountered those issues then is an historical construct. My
entire life has been influenced by that crucial experience,
but I am no longer the person I was then. When people ask
what changes I had observed in Dolpa recently (where I had
done Ph.D. research after the Peace Corps), trekking around
that remote and difficult terrain after a 42 year absence, the
answer is easy: The major difference is that I'm no longer 28
years old.

I am an "insider" trying to distance myself by
simultaneously assuming the role of an "outsider." The
resulting hybrid picture I draw borrows from both these
worlds.

The flip side of being observationally protean is the
necessity to remind myself that I wear the same blinders as
everyone else. The need to capture the "native voice" (i.e.,
ours) in assessing the events we participated in and created,
whether we are, or see ourselves, as agents of cultural
imperialism or not, must be tempered by the same hard,
cold facts an impartial observer would have to confront
and assess. Whether viewed from the inside or the outside,
the stubborn empirical reality is that we were witnessing
the consolidation of a new global society. That we were
contributing to the construction of that society is seen in our
observations and reflections, which comprise the core of this
book. The musings it contains are only fragments, but such
fragments from wherever they are found do come together
to create a world of global connections.[28]

Despite my privileged insider position—although
the usefulness of the insider/outsider dichotomy can be
overdrawn[29]—the interviews were revealing and fascinating
beyond my most optimistic expectations. Although I
thought I knew my fellow Volunteers quite well, and
some of them I thought I knew very well, not a single
interview ended without my learning of some experience,

sentiment, observation, activity, or thought that was totally unexpected—e.g., that what I thought was a success someone else thought was a failure, or that some policy that I thought was working someone else thought was foolish, or what I thought was key to achievement others thought was irrelevant. The lesson I learned from these conversations is the chastening one that I knew, from first principles, much less than I thought I knew.

In addition to basic data about education, ethnic/religious origin, marriage, divorce, children, occupation, and age (the effects and perceptions most of us, in our 20s, experienced are certainly different from those that the few in our group who were of middle-age or older experienced), I also asked more open-ended questions about motivations for joining the Peace Corps, type and location of assignment, religious views, social class, and political inclinations. The stories and reflections often reveal total role reversals, over time—from farmer to state agricultural bureaucrat, from home economics teacher to international consultant, from high school graduate to Ph.D. In other words, these are stories of lives forever transformed.

There are also larger reflections about the experience: that we learned much more than we taught (everyone was emphatic on that point); that the rewards we frequently experienced vastly outweighed the travails we occasionally felt; that Nepalese traits that irritated us at the time (what we experienced as excessive adherence to tradition, or attention to human and family relations, or reluctance to replace old ways that did work with new ideas that might work), seem understandable, and even admirable in retrospect. This is no doubt due partially to the wisdom of our advanced age, which would have eventually caught up with us anyway, but also to the shift in cultural values which was affected by our intimate encounter with a different way of thinking. That change would not have occurred without experiencing Nepalese life up close and personal.

We found ourselves beginning to exoticize some values so fundamental to our own culture that we hadn't questioned them, such as the unchallenged importance of efficiency and production. We were not the result of a post-1960s cultural shift toward appreciation of cultural difference, but, being products of the 1950s, right in the thick of it.

Finally, although I share with my subjects the same restricted vision of what happened to us, my role as anthropologist casts me in what at least some of my fellow Volunteers will likely regard as a very odd light. For almost all of us, what one Volunteer later called "the golden years in Nepal" seems beyond discussion, let alone critique. Orientalists? Imperialists? Even agents of the military-industrial-diplomatic complex? He must be joking, they're liable to say. But the skeptic's scold must be faced, if only to be stared down.

Perhaps the critical stance will not seem all that alien after all, though, since the entire two-year overseas stint turned most of the group, inadvertently, into quasi-anthropologists anyway. Our change in thinking was brought about directly by the Peace Corps experience in Nepal; simple survival and sanity required continuous, unremitting attempts to understand how an unfamiliar way of life worked. Thus, this preceded the movement toward cultural analyses and emphasis on difference that developed later with the civil rights movement and popular promotion of the idea of cultural relativism, which had always been part of the core of anthropology.

Conversations about why things were the way they were—such discussions were a recurrent if unintended consequence of finding ourselves yanked out of our comfort zones and inserted into the turbulent maelstrom of globalization. A frequently evoked epiphany that weaves its way into these remembrances is the revelation, and indeed the insistence, that the world consists not only of other nations, governments, technologies, economies, agricultural practices, and educational systems, but also, more fundamentally, pervasively, and powerfully, of other cultures. An anthropologist could not ask for more.

2

STARTING FROM SCRATCH

Beginnings

One of the first countries to request Volunteers after the
Peace Corps came into existence was Nepal. There was
speculation at the time that the U.S. exerted pressure on the
government of Nepal (and probably the governments of
other countries) to "request" Volunteers. After all, it would
be embarrassing if the U.S. offered to send Volunteers to
other countries but could find no takers—the diplomatic
equivalent of throwing a party to which no one shows up.
As recipients of "foreign aid" from the U.S., governments
of poor countries like Nepal would be vulnerable to such
pressure, but there is no documentary evidence that this
was the case. Without relevant documentation, speculation
about such diplomatic maneuvering can be neither
confirmed nor discredited.

In any case, the bureaucratic wheels were set in motion
to send a group of Volunteers to Nepal (groups were also
being sent to Ghana, Nigeria, Tanzania, Philippines, and
Columbia in the first year.) Recruiting procedures were set
in place, and Peace Corps advance staff went to Nepal to
make preliminary arrangements with various Ministries of
what was then called HMG (His Majesty's Government)*
for field assignments. George Washington University
was contracted to provide training in job skills, American
studies, health, and Nepali language and culture. Outward

---

* Most of the royal family was assassinated in 2001; the monarchy was
  abolished in 2008. The country is now known officially as the Federal
  Democratic Republic of Nepal.

Bound, just getting started in Colorado, was asked to mount a program of mountain training, on the somewhat speculative theory that such preparation would be required to survive in a predominantly mountainous country like Nepal.[*]

In addition to Volunteers, administrative staff needed to be recruited to anchor what would become the Peace Corps office in Kathmandu. The Peace Corps was run by non-Volunteer "adult" leaders in each country. In the case of Nepal, the Peace Corps started at the top by selecting as its Representative there Robert Bates, an English teacher at Exeter Academy in New Hampshire, who had been working part-time as a consultant to the Peace Corps since late 1961. Bates in turn recruited a philosopher at Oregon State University, Willi Unsoeld, as his Deputy.

In addition to their academic credentials, both were well known, in international mountaineering circles, for their records of pioneering and daring ascents in the Himalayan and Karakoram mountain ranges, among other places. Bates and Unsoeld seemed to personify the personality type—action-oriented intellectuals—that fit perfectly with President Kennedy's view of vigorous liberalism that would win over the Third World. Moreover, by contrast with the New Frontiersmen staffing Washington bureaucracies, they were adventurers willing and eager to go to one of the most remote places on the planet to promote progress in the world; in a phrase waiting to be invented then but popular later in the century, they not only talked the talk but walked the walk. They, and the Peace Corps generally, stood in sharp contrast with the negative image of the Ugly American common at the time.[30]

American secretarial staff was also eventually recruited, to be supplemented later by Nepali employees, to fill out the Kathmandu office of the Peace Corps.

---

[*] This is a little like arguing that Volunteers assigned to tropical, cyclone-prone countries like the Philippines should receive training in Louisiana, but such training was never proposed.

Why Volunteers Volunteered

At an end-of-service evaluation held May 12-17, 1964, just before Volunteers left Nepal, a questionnaire was administered that listed twelve reasons people might have had for joining the Peace Corps:

1) to gain intercultural experience
2) to teach
3) to act on belief in the Peace Corps
4) to work with people
5) to further a career
6) to gain personal satisfaction
7) to create close, person-to-person relationships
8) to change the American image abroad
9) to learn or gain general experience
10) to build a better world
11) to apply previous intercultural experience
12) to apply specific skills or knowledge

None of these reasons could be described as explicitly answering "Kennedy's call," but most are not inconsistent with it. In my interviews with Volunteers decades later, however, I found few Volunteers who spoke in terms of any of these twelve reasons, or of answering Kennedy's call. As we shall see below, most had other things on their minds.

Very few of the Volunteers in that first group wanted specifically to go to Nepal. The few who did want to go to Nepal requested an assignment there because of specific interests, acquired in idiosyncratic ways—e.g., from reading old National Geographic magazines, seeing a Lowell Thomas film, reading James Hilton's novel, *Lost Horizon* (Hilton 1934) or Toni Hagen's *Nepal* (Hagen 1961), or simply having heard of Hillary and Tenzing's ascent of Everest a few years earlier.

But for the great majority of Volunteers who drew Nepal as an assignment, it was for no reason other than the luck of the draw. The overwhelming majority of the applicants who were offered the opportunity to go to Nepal had little or no idea where Nepal was. When Mickey Veich got his assignment letter, he said, perhaps not entirely tongue-in-cheek, "Like everyone else I ran for the map of Africa." Hal Christensen's reaction on being informed of his selection was, "I didn't even know there *was* a Nepal!"

Mickey's and Hal's reactions were not atypical. After being offered their assignments for Nepal, the first reaction of most was to try to find maps that would show where Nepal was. In those pre-Internet days, this often involved trips to nearby libraries to consult an atlas. Ralph Hambrick later reflected on the irony that he didn't know where Nepal was, and then when he went to Nepal, he met people who didn't know where America was. The ignorance was mutual and reciprocal—exactly the kind of witlessness the Peace Corps was designed to remedy.

Lee Tuveson recalled how, when deciding whether to go to Nepal, he remembered Yogi Berra's advice: "When you come to a fork in the road, take it!" He thought that while we cannot control many events, like natural disasters, in exercising choice of careers and spouses we do exercise control—we can choose which fork in the road to take. We make these decisions as individuals, but the consequences of our choices are often unpredictable and involve commitments that, once undertaken, are seldom reversible.

On Memorial Day 1962, having just finished his B.A. degree from North Central College in Naperville, IL, Lee was spending time at home with his family when Western Union called. There was a telegram from Peace Corps Washington inviting him to Peace Corps training for Naples. Lee was mystified. During the spring he had taken a number of Civil Service exams at the local post office on Saturdays. He didn't have any particular job prospects as graduation approached, so government employment was at least a possibility. In addition to whatever other government jobs he had applied for, he had also inadvertently applied to the Peace Corps. When he went to Western Union to pick up the message, he saw that it did not say Naples, but Nepal.

That only intensified the mystery since no one in his family knew where Nepal was. His father took out a world atlas, searched the index, and found Nepal. Standing over his shoulder Lee watched as he flipped the pages until he finally found the map. "There are no roads! Why would anyone want to go to such a remote, godforsaken place?" his father asked. He was obviously not impressed with the Peace Corps offer. Lee's older brother took him aside and counseled otherwise. He believed it would be an interesting opportunity and regretted not taking a break from his own academic pursuits earlier. A few days later Lee was on his way to the training program in Washington.

Similarly, Bob Rhoades, who had grown up on an Oklahoma farm, upon receiving his telegram was resigned to going to Italy. It wasn't until he pulled out an encyclopedia at the library that he discovered that Nepal was another country entirely, about which very little was known. This prompted him to begin thinking that it would be more interesting than Naples.

What sorts of considerations prompted these young people to volunteer—whether for the Peace Corps in general (true of almost all of these first Nepal Volunteers) or for Nepal in particular (true of a very small sub-set of them)?

One way to approach the question of motivation for joining the Peace Corps is to consider the rewards that might be expected. What were they? If anyone thought of possible financial rewards, that idea had a short shelf-life, with the possible exception of one or two who were unemployed and with no particularly attractive job prospects. It was made clear from the beginning that Peace Corps Volunteers would be provided only with housing plus a monthly living allowance roughly equivalent to what our Nepalese counterparts would be receiving.

The monthly living allowance in Nepal was established at Rs. 350 (350 Nepali rupees, as distinguished from the more valuable Indian rupee), which at that time was equivalent to about U.S. $46. Whether this amount was adequate, insufficient, or excessive, depended on local circumstances. For someone teaching in a boarding school, (as I did for a while), who was provided a room and dining privileges to eat along with the students and staff in the common dining hall, there were no expenses other than what one might spend on personal items such as toothpaste or a copy of Time Magazine, if it could be found (in Kathmandu only, and then only sporadically). For someone in a rural area where items such as tinned food, which could only be carried in on a porter's back, were relatively expensive, $46 might require a tighter budget.

In my first assignment, in the city of Bhaktapur, eight miles east of Kathmandu, my expenses included: laundry, $1.78/month; crank-started bus to Kathmandu, $0.06 one way (except on holidays, when the price went up somewhat); cook, for three meals/day, $1.00/week ($4.00 split four ways with my three roommates); food, about $10/week; haircut, $0.10. The Peace Corps paid the rent on our house ($30/month). Our landlord had been willing to rent the house (a substantial, multi-storied one) for $14, but started the bargaining by asking for $34, and was quite pleased when the Peace Corps countered, naively, with an offer of $30.

But while our living allowance was pegged at par with what our counterparts were paid, there were several differences to consider between remuneration for Nepalis and Americans. For example, our counterparts generally had families to feed, whereas we did not. Moreover, in the case of the few married couples in our group, both husband and wife worked and therefore received two salaries. There were other Volunteer perks, such as up-to-date medical care, at no cost to themselves, from the Peace Corps doctor, Mark Rhine, a graduate of Harvard Medical School who was assigned by the U. S. Public Health Service to minister to the health needs of Nepal Volunteers.

Volunteers were also issued amenities such as a footlocker of paperback books, which contained various popular genres, including a healthy representation of Americana. In addition, travel expenses were covered to attend occasional Volunteer conferences in Kathmandu. Such considerations as these prompted the following observation, made by an unnamed government official and quoted in a 1964 issue of the Nepal Peace Corps newsletter:

"Though in theory Peace Corps Volunteers are supposed to live on the same economic level as Nepalis doing the same work, this is not true in practice. The Nepali has to support his family and save for the future, while the Volunteer can spend his earning on his own comforts."

But Nepalis also possessed certain advantages not available to the Volunteers. Nepalese families could provide various kinds of support, including financial support, such as ownership of houses, land, or other forms of property, to which Volunteers did not have access. Of course they also had extensive family and kinship ties they could draw on to provide support, financial or otherwise, when it was needed. Volunteers had only each other, and they were all financially on the same playing field.

The most significant difference in income level derived from the fact that Nepalese teachers could and did supplement their salaries with "private tuitions"—i.e., tutoring individual students to help them pass their exams. This was an important income supplement unavailable to Volunteers, because we didn't know the system well enough to provide tutoring, and even if we did, it would have been improper for us to moonlight in this way, outside of the official school system.

In addition to the $46 monthly living allowance, each Volunteer was given, upon return to the U.S., a "termination allowance" of $75 for each month of service completed. The logic of the termination allowance, which amounted to $1800 for those who had completed two years of service, including the training period, was to provide Volunteers a bridge to cross over and enable them to reenter American society, whether that reentry led to further education or a job.

For anyone inclined towards the traditional American goal of seeking one's fortune, therefore, the Peace Corps experience had little appeal. At the end of one's Peace Corps tenure there was little material gain to show for it: almost no money, no credits one might apply towards a college or graduate degree, and precious few recommendation letters to accompany a job or college application. Volunteers could not look forward to importing material goods to the U.S. from their countries of assignment other than the odd souvenir and, perhaps, one or more of several types of intestinal parasite (amoebas, giardia, round worms, hook worms, and pin worms, to name some of them) and, in a few instances, a lingering case of malaria or hepatitis. So, apart from the lure of communicable diseases, what did attract these people to the Peace Corps in 1962?

Part of the explanation for joining the Peace Corps lay in the nature of the recruitment process. This consisted partly of clever advertisements showing enticing graphics, emphasizing "the hardest job you'll ever love," and claiming to provide what William James once called "the moral equivalent of war."[31] The unspoken supposition was that to remove violence from people's lives would require a romance of peace equal to that of war.[32] In addition to saturation public advertising, educational institutions were also comprehensively canvassed—high schools as well as colleges and universities. Brochures and applications were easily available, and speakers were provided, some of them Hollywood or sports celebrities whom Sargent Shriver (Director of the Peace Corps and brother-in-law of President Kennedy) had recruited to raise the Peace Corps profile in the public eye.

In the case of Nepal the process was somewhat atypical because of the profession and character of its first Representative, Robert Bates. As Representative (the equivalent of "Director" in other government agencies), Bob was the ultimate in-country authority over all aspects of the Peace Corps operation: Volunteer assignments, personnel policies, relations with HMG, with the Peace Corps office in Washington, and with the rest of the American establishment in Nepal. Bob had spent a lifetime in secondary education teaching English at Exeter Academy in New Hampshire. In the fall of 1961 he had become a consultant to the Peace Corps, and in early 1962 was appointed Representative for Nepal.

Starting close to home, he immediately set out to recruit

promising students he had known at Exeter, and then moved on to New England universities where he travelled to meet prospective Volunteers during recruiting trips. Many who had never previously heard of Nepal became excited by Bob's description (he had travelled there before) of its natural beauty, friendly people, and fascinating culture.

Of the 70 Volunteers who eventually went to Nepal in Fall 1962, twelve had heard about the program directly through the good offices of Bob Bates. All of these twelve had New England roots. While they may not have known much, or indeed anything, about Nepal to begin with, Bob's recruiting pitch was geared specifically to Nepal. In these cases, the hook worked, as the following narratives show.

Mark Schroeder had been a student of Bob's at Exeter. After graduating in dairy science from the University of Vermont, Mark began farming in northern Vermont. The big modernization of farms going on at the time meant that he had to buy a bulk milk tank, but such an investment would put him out of business (as it was putting other small farmers like him out of business). As an alternative, Mark investigated an overseas assignment with the Quakers, but their assignments were all in equatorial Africa, and he couldn't stand the heat. Just at this time Bob Bates called and asked if he'd like to go to Nepal with the Peace Corps. The timing was perfect. The woman he was dating, Suki Saltonstall, applied too, and they were married fairly soon after they arrived in Nepal.

Rolf Goetze had also attended Exeter; he and his wife, Julie, had independently decided on the Peace Corps. They had listened to Kennedy's inaugural speech and were much struck by the idealism inherent in the Peace Corps idea. They applied and were offered jobs in Malaysia, which wanted architects (Rolf was an architect), but Rolf's father, a colleague of Bob Bates at Exeter, said he'd heard that Bob might be taking a group to Nepal. Rolf had learned about Nepal over the years from National Geographic articles, and the appealing idea of going to a place without roads (Nepal) instead of one with roads (Malaysia) led to their choice of Nepal.

Doug Bingham, a senior at Yale, had wondered only vaguely about the Peace Corps, thinking it wasn't for him, but Bob knew about Doug through his family, and convinced him to sign up.

Similarly, Peter Farquhar had known Bob and Gail Bates through his parents and common mountaineering associations. Bob asked Peter, then finishing his M.A. in geography at the University of Colorado, if he would like to become involved in the training program being set up in Puerto Rico. Peter said yes, but when Bob was named Representative for Nepal early in 1962, he called Peter back and asked if he'd like to be a Volunteer in Nepal instead. Peter's instant answer was, again, yes. He had learned about geography in the classroom, but now he was ready to see how geography looked and worked in the real world.

For some Volunteers, the Peace Corps was an alternative to military service. Peter Grote, wondering what to do after graduating from Harvard, started investigating the Marine Corps and got as far as passing the physical. The Peace Corps was also much in the air, though, and a mountaineering friend of Bob's told Peter that Bob had just been appointed Director for Nepal. In Peter's eyes, that was no contest, so he immediately called Bob and became one of his first recruits.

Ralph Hambrick's decision to join the Peace Corps was entirely whimsical. He was beginning to feel burned out in his third year at Dartmouth and decided to drop out for a while. He needed to do something dramatic, to allay his parents' concerns about dropping out, and decided to let his fate be determined by a coin toss: heads, Peace Corps; tails, Marine Corps. He had no idealistic notions, and his motivation was to see the world, but he was relieved that heads won. He applied, and then hitchhiked to Florida, where he was contacted by the Peace Corps and found he'd been offered an assignment in Nepal. Like many others, he had to check an atlas to see where it was.

Bob knew most of these applicants personally, or knew about them, through family and school connections. He eventually recruited six more Volunteers studying at New England universities. Les Gile, Dick Murphy and his wife

Becky, Dave Towle, Beverly Fogg, and Bill Carter were all studying at the University of New Hampshire.

Les was in his third year as an agricultural major. He had not yet ventured out of New England, but he had always been curious about how other people lived. He'd heard the general buzz about the Peace Corps—through advertisements, Kennedy's speech, and arguments about whether it should be established or not. When Bob Bates came on a University of New Hampshire recruiting trip, Les was very impressed with his enthusiasm and immediately applied for Nepal.

Like Les, Dick and Becky Murphy were already interested in the Peace Corps before meeting Bob Bates, but Bob was the deciding factor in their decision to request Nepal. They were both finishing their degrees at the University of New Hampshire when the Peace Corps came along. Dick felt that he had been taking all his life—from his parents, from his university—and he wanted to give something back to his country. He was majoring in agricultural engineering (his wife was studying occupational therapy), and his physical chemistry professor, who was the Peace Corps liaison on campus, asked him to arrange a meeting on campus for Bob Bates. Dick and Becky had already filled out their applications, except for their preferred country, but Bob's presentation sold them, so they went out to their car, got their applications, and handed them to Bob. Training was to begin in two weeks, and they said they wanted to be posted as a married couple. They drove to Becky's parents' house, woke them at 1:30 a.m. and said they needed to be married in a hurry.

One of Dave Towle's first serious thoughts about the Peace Corps came from the knowledge that an ex-girlfriend was going to join, and it sounded like a good idea. Later, Dave didn't hear about Bob's campus visit till the day after it took place, but he called up Bob, who said, "Come on over, and we'll chat." As he did in most of these cases, Bob hand carried the applications to Washington for immediate consideration.

Probably the most compelling example of Bob's recruiting effectiveness was Beverly Fogg, who hadn't considered the Peace Corps prior to his talk. Beverly was a senior, "taking classes and not going to class," when she saw a sign advertising a talk on Nepal. She had always been fascinated by Everest—wanted to climb it, she said—so she went to the talk and heard about the Peace Corps group leaving in a couple of weeks. When she told Bob she wanted to go, he said that it was too late, and everyone had already been selected. Being insistent, she argued that since he was the leader he could squeeze her in, so he told her to come to his house for tea the next day to try to convince him. He then partially relented, saying that if she brought a couple of letters of recommendation with her he would take them to Washington the day after that. So she asked some professors for letters of recommendation, thinking they would at least be glad to be rid of her, but she did surreptitiously open the sealed envelopes just to be sure. Luckily, what she saw made her confident she would be accepted.

Four other New Englanders applied, but without a connection to Bob. Bill Carter was studying horticulture at the University of New Hampshire, and heard from one of his professors that the Peace Corps needed horticulturalists in Nepal. That was enough for him.

Ron Elliot was sitting around in Keene Teacher's College in New Hampshire, wondering how he and his roommate could get out of the country and go somewhere without any money. They heard about the Peace Corps, got applications at the Post Office, and filled them out. Ron was assigned to Nepal, his roommate to the Philippines.

Mac Odell, a resident of the greater Boston area, had taken a year off from Princeton to go to Denmark to learn how to build boats. He was intrigued by the bigger world out there, and by the time he came back and finished his Asian history major the Peace Corps had come along. While clearly intrigued by Kennedy's call, he was too busy to attend a talk on the new Peace Corps Nepal program given at Rutgers nearby, but some friends went, came back ecstatic, and told him he had to apply. He did and got accepted for British Honduras, which was a shock because he had requested Nepal. But he tracked down the

Rutgers recruiter, asked what had gone wrong, and got his assignment switched to Nepal.

Peter Prindle had graduated from Tufts University and was in his first year of medical school at the University of Vermont when an older man—someone in his nineties, he thought—gave a talk about the Peace Corps. Peter had been interested in Nepal from reading National Geographic magazines, so that's the country he applied for.

The narratives of these New Englanders show that the question of what motivated people to join the Peace Corps has many answers. Because of Bates' recruiting efforts, these New Englanders were disproportionately interested in Nepal. Certainly some, like the Goetzes and the Murphys, were inspired to "answer Kennedy's call," but others had reasons of their own, and every person's decision was to some extent idiosyncratic.

Apart from what I'm calling here the seventeen New Englanders, the other 53 Volunteers hailed from all over the country. The largest number—23—came from the Midwest, many of them with agricultural backgrounds. Eleven came from California, four from other western states, six from the south, four from the non-New England east coast, three from the Pacific northwest, and one from Hawaii. Lacking any direct contact with Bob Bates, the proportion of these who had no idea of what or where Nepal was when they applied was higher.

A very few of these non-New Englanders applied because they wanted to go to Nepal, but the overwhelming majority applied to the Peace Corps for unpredictable, non-Nepal related reasons. As both the New England and the following examples show, some were nudged by a friend or teacher, some were in search of adventure, and some wanted to travel, see the world, or see Mt. Everest. Others were turned down for a job they had applied for. Some just wanted a change in their lives, and wanted nothing more than to do something different from whatever they had been doing.

Of all the non-New Englanders, I believe I was the only one for whom going to Nepal was the compelling and deciding factor in joining the Peace Corps. I was a senior at Princeton University contemplating graduate school in anthropology at the University of Chicago the following fall. I was also in contact with the Peace Corps, who wanted to know if I would like a summer job with the training camp in Puerto Rico. When asked if I would be interested in a regular assignment as a Volunteer I said no; I was only available for the summer—"unless," I added as an afterthought, "there were a group going to Nepal." I thought there was virtually no chance of that happening, but when it did, Chicago was willing to defer my admission to graduate school for two years, and off I went to Nepal.

Thus I was one of the few whose interest in Nepal predated the creation of the Peace Corps. Why? Climbing as high as I could in the trees in my front yard in Kentucky may have had something to do with it. For reasons I've never fully understood, but other mountaineers understand immediately, I had always loved being high in the mountains (in spite of, or perhaps because of, a fear of heights). My father was a geologist and loved the outdoors, but no one else in my family or community shared my interest, which was confirmed when I went to a summer camp (Cheley) near Rocky Mountain National Park and climbed Longs Peak (I repeated the ascent with my son 43 years later). That was the summer of 1953, the year Sir Edmund Hillary and Tenzing Norgay made the first ascent of Mt. Everest. I was 13 years old at the time and thought, well, now I'll never make the first ascent of Everest. I remember the rumor making the rounds at the camp, which seems preposterous in retrospect, that it had been climbed by an illiterate tribesman and therefore may not have really been climbed at all.

In any case I had long been fascinated by the Himalayas as the highest mountain range on the planet. But there was something else. Some years before I had read and been completely captivated by James Hilton's novel *Lost Horizon*, and its description of Shangri-La in some enchanting but unspecified location in the Himalayas. I was somewhat disenchanted, in the way a young man seeking meaning in life can be, with American society and wondered if there really were a Shangri-La somewhere, and if there were, if it might be in Nepal. If it was there, I wanted to go find it.

Bert Puchtler said that like all significant events in his life, going to Nepal came about more by accident than by intention—yet for Bert, too, his decision to join was more about deciding to go to Nepal than about joining the Peace Corps *per se*. He was just finishing his M.A. in modern European history at Berkeley (his B.A. was from Wesleyan) and wondering what would happen next. Mercifully, he added, it had been suggested that he conclude his academic career. Then he got a call from a female staffer in the White House, who said "Bert, the Peace Corps is looking for rugged people to go to Nepal, and I think you'd fit the bill." Bert says she didn't know that his male friends called him Poopout Puchtler. He found two wilted National Geographics, a history of the Ranas, and Toni Hagen's book on Nepal. The latter did the trick.

Mimi Smith was far more deliberate in her choice, both to enter the Peace Corps and to request Nepal. She was a senior at the University of North Carolina in Chapel Hill, in 1960, when she heard that Kennedy had proposed a Peace Corps-type organization during a campaign speech at the University of Michigan. She found out every way she could, by writing and asking many people, how to apply for such a thing. She finally did get an application and sent it in, and was told that they would be in touch with her.

While driving across the country to California with a friend, after graduation, she phoned her parents in her once-weekly call (as she had promised to do), and was told that she had gotten a telegram telling her to report for training for a program in the Philippines within nine days. She said that for all sorts of logistical reasons that would be totally impossible. She continued her trip to California and then returned to Washington, where her family, who were conservative military people (her grandfather had been Commandant of the Marine Corps), took a rather dim view of her going to the Philippines with the Peace Corps. So she made a deal with them: She would find a job at Peace Corps headquarters in Washington, and then after a year if it still looked sensible enough she would apply again to become a Volunteer.

She was interviewed by Bill Moyers, who was impressed that she had been accepted as a Volunteer, and she spent the next year working for him. While living in Washington, Marjorie Michelmore, a Volunteer in Nigeria who was sent home early because of an infamous postcard she wrote describing what she regarded as primitive conditions there (and which was very bad public relations for the Peace Corps), came back to Washington and ended up living with Mimi for a while.

While working at Peace Corps headquarters she began to scout out possible countries to apply to. At first there were only two or three countries available. She wanted to go to Afghanistan, but was told they wanted only professional people and only 13 of those, so then she chose Nepal, which was almost as unknown. This was critical because she wanted to go to a place that she knew the least about. Working at Peace Corps headquarters, she was able to engineer things so that she got the assignment she wanted, rather than being assigned at random, as were most Volunteers to Nepal.

Far more common than Mimi's engineering of her assignment to Nepal were Volunteers who were randomly assigned there, often after initially expecting or, in some cases, hoping for a different assignment. Ken Van Sickle was in his first year at Ellendale State Teachers College in his hometown in North Dakota when he met a man who was going to be on the Peace Corps staff in Bolivia and told Ken he could get him into a program there. Ken filed an application, but then an invitation for Nepal arrived, and although he still could have gone to Bolivia, he thought, after he had dug up some old National Geographics, that Nepal sounded more interesting.

Likewise, Al Champney ended up in Nepal partially via what appeared to be an administrative error. Al was studying for an M.A. in economics at the University of Michigan. For lack of anything better to do he applied to the Foreign Service and the Peace Corps. He was rejected from the former because of bad eyesight, but a telegram from the

Peace Corps offered him an assignment in Belize. The follow-up letter that arrived by regular mail mentioned nothing about Belize and offered, inconsistently and paradoxically, an assignment in Nepal. No explanation was made of the discrepancy, so Al took it on himself to accept the offer made in the letter rather than the one made in the telegram.

Mel Kinder and his wife Dottie also ended up in Nepal in spite of a different preference. Mel was finishing his B.A. at UCLA when the Peace Corps publicity reached him and Dottie. They applied almost immediately, for Arab countries, and Morocco specifically, because Mel had not only majored in Middle Eastern history but had studied Arabic. Since Dottie didn't know French, however, they were offered Nepal. They'd heard about Nepal from a Lowell Thomas film, and the only book in the library on Nepal was Toni Hagen's *Nepal*, in German. They got enough of it translated to realize that Nepal was a place they wanted to go to.

More numerous than Volunteers inspired to go to Nepal were those inspired by President Kennedy. The interest of Helen Carter, from California, was piqued by the thought that she could answer Kennedy's call, but also satisfy her interest in India, which was initiated by Jacqueline Kennedy's visit there. Thus, she was inspired not only by the President's speech, but by the President's wife.

For some, Kennedy's speech was all it took. Dave Kollasch was four years out of high school in Iowa, working as an electronic technician in a local manufacturing plant, when he heard Kennedy's inaugural speech. About a year later he applied and was offered Nepal.

For others, Kennedy's influence was more direct. Mickey Veich was studying at Compton Junior College in Compton, CA when Bobby and Teddy Kennedy visited the campus. As student body vice president Mickey was charged with escorting them around. One of them told Mickey that he "sounded like the kind of kid who should be in the Peace Corps," and Mickey said, "Tell me more about it." They said Sargent Shriver, whom Mickey had never heard of, would get in contact with him. The next thing he knew someone on Shriver's staff called him. Mickey filled out the application and then got a telegram from Shriver saying he had been selected for Nepal (not Africa, which was what he thought at first).

Bob Murphy also had a "Kennedy connection". He had graduated from Wisconsin State University in River Falls and was working for an insurance company in San Francisco when he went to hear John Kennedy give a speech in which he mentioned the Peace Corps. After the speech Bob asked Kennedy, directly, when he could join. Kennedy was a little flustered, but turned him over to an aide, and several months later Bob was in training at George Washington University. He had heard a little about Nepal because of Hillary and Tenzing, but not much more than that.

Flemming Heegaard had an association with Kennedy, but it was not what he thought it was at first. He was in graduate school at San Jose State working on a master's degree in clinical psychology. Peace Corps was in the air so he took the test. He had forgotten all about it when he got a telegram from President Kennedy—he was so naïve, he said, he thought the President had personally written to him.

Jane Stevens was a freshman at the University of Illinois when Kennedy came through on a campaign swing just after his University of Michigan speech about the Peace Corps. This caught her fancy, and she sent in a postcard indicating interest. The next year she was offered an assignment in Nepal, somewhat to the concern of her Midwestern Republican family, who happened to live down the street from the leading conservative Republican of his day, Everett Dirksen, who was minority leader of the Senate.

Bernie Snoyer, originally from Holland, had just become an American citizen when he heard Kennedy's speech, but he was thinking more about travel than anything else. Another part of his motivation, he said, was that he knew too many Dutchmen and wanted the chance to get to know more Americans, which he thought he could do in the Peace Corps.

Bob Shrader, from rural West Virginia, heard Kennedy's speech about doing something for your country. Having grown up on a farm, he thought he could contribute something in agricultural education, and then, as a high-school senior, he got one of the cards they sent out to students. He filled it out, sent it in, jumped through the ensuing administrative hoops, and ultimately received an assignment for Nepal.

Bernie and Bob, in addition to being inspired by Kennedy, display two other important motivations for many of the Nepal I Volunteers: a desire for travel and adventure on the one hand, and an idealistic desire to help people on the other. Glenda Warren had always wanted to be of service to people and to work or travel abroad, so the Peace Corps was a perfect combination of Glenda's interests and the Peace Corps mission. She was studying home economics at Langston University in Oklahoma when a Peace Corps recruiter came to the campus. To increase her chances of acceptance she said she would go to any country that needed her skills.

Similarly, Nick Cibrario wanted to help people; he was also bored and wanted an adventure. He was in his third year of college at La Crosse State, in Wisconsin. He was much influenced by the books of three authors: Louis Fischer's *Mahatma Gandhi*, Tom Dooley's *The Night they Burned the Mountain*, and Albert Schweitzer's *Out of My Life and Thought*. He wanted to go to Asia to see what was going on over there, and the Peace Corps gave him that chance.

Carl Jorgensen was finishing up his math major at Harvard and realized that he needed a break before graduate school. The Peace Corps appealed because it seemed like a way to experience another culture and do something positive without being patronizing about it.

Another mathematician was Mike Frame, finishing his senior year at Carleton College in Minnesota. He wanted to see the world, heard about the Peace Corps in the news, applied, and that was that. He ended up spending most of the rest of his life in Nepal, working in a variety of positions for Peace Corps and USAID before starting his own restaurant in Kathmandu and, later, a hotel in Pokhara.

For a couple of Volunteers, the desire to help and do good was bound together with their religious beliefs and background. Peace Corps identity was so strong that none made the slightest attempt to proselytize; they were as likely as any other Volunteers to develop an interest in indigenous religions. Hal Christensen was a senior at St. Olaf College in Minnesota. He applied for an opening in Greece with the World Council of Churches but was not accepted for the position. He was not particularly interested in the Peace Corps, but when a recruiter came to St. Olaf, Hal filled out an application. When he later was offered the chance to go to Nepal, he decided to take it.

Dave Sears said that a history of missionaries in his family was an influence when, in his second year at South Western Missouri State College, he heard about the Peace Corps through a college friend who had gone to the Philippines as a Volunteer. At the same time, Nepal was also an opportunity for adventure, and to grow up a little. Many years later Dave enrolled in and graduated from a seminary, but his agricultural work in Nepal had nothing to do with religion.

While he was not motivated by religion, Ralph Teague also credited a family history of service in making his decision. Ralph was born in Idaho but moved to Walla Walla, Washington when he was in the fourth grade, and had been involved in various kinds of community service there due to the guidance of his parents. He left home to go to the University of Washington, but kept grounded by association with the West League Foundation, a community action group. When the Peace Corps came along he decided to apply, but in the meantime he went on an international work camp in Brazil for a month and a half. Then a telegram from the Peace Corps arrived asking him to join the Nepal group.

For several Volunteers, the desire for adventure trumped idealism. Jerry Young was studying at Western Michigan University when a friend walked into his dorm room and said he'd just heard that President Kennedy was starting a new organization called the Peace Corps, and that you could take the exam at the post office that coming Saturday. He said, "Let's take the test and see where it goes." As it turned out, Jerry's friend wasn't accepted but Jerry was.

Jerry's motivation, he said, was grounded not in idealism but in a desire to seek adventure and to see the world after growing up in a rural farm area in southern Michigan. When he was invited in 1961 to go to Africa for the Peace Corps he was traveling in Europe and didn't receive the letter. The following year he didn't request Nepal; as in most of the other cases, it was just the luck of the draw—what later Nepali friends might have labeled fate.

Bob Rhoades was studying at Oklahoma State University in order to become an agricultural extension officer. In college he had heard a little about the rest of the world and wanted to see more of it. His brother was in Germany in the army and hated it. He saw Vietnam on the horizon and wrote to Bob urging him to look into the Peace Corps. He was also caught up in the spirit of the thing, as were many, he said, who wanted to do something good for the world. So he applied and received a telegram in his mobile home, that he had been accepted for Nepal.

Larry Wolfe was attending Riverside City College in California at the same time he was serving as a communications specialist at Norton Air Force Base. Peace Corps recruiters came to the college campus looking for volunteers for Borneo. Larry applied, expecting to go to Borneo, but was assigned to Nepal instead.

Bob Proctor's mother showed him a Peace Corps ad in the local newspaper in Santa Fe—perhaps with good reason, he said, since he had just quit graduate school at the University of Chicago, and the draft board was breathing down his neck. He applied and then finished off his M.A. degree in biology. His earlier correspondence with the Peace Corps had produced an assignment in British Honduras, which suited Bob fine, especially since he had just spent time bumming around Mexico and liked life south of the border. The switch to Nepal was totally unexpected. He had hardly heard of the country, beyond a Lowell Thomas film. He arrived in Washington less than enthusiastic, but glad at least to be doing something rather than nothing.

Some Volunteers cited the Peace Corps as an answer to the problem of getting a job. Joyce Thorkelson was a senior

Geography major at Fresno State with rather uninteresting job prospects, so she pursued the Peace Corps possibility. One of her fellow majors had already left for Columbia in the Peace Corps, and as bits and pieces of his experience filtered back, it all became more exciting. She applied for Southeast Asia, thinking of Thailand, but she was offered Nepal. Her mother was somewhat adventurous and very excited over all this, but her father thought she should get a job at the post office.

George Peck graduated with a physics major at the University of Colorado. His attempt to get a job with the Bureau of Standards in Boulder failed because of a bad reference from a summer job with a forest service trail crew, so he joined the Peace Corps instead.

Bill Clayton was finishing up his B.S. in agricultural economics at Clemson University and looking for something to do after graduation that was attractive and not too taxing. He heard about the Peace Corps on the news, applied, was accepted for Nepal, and then, again, went to the library to find out what part of the world it was in.

Several Volunteers described stumbling into the Peace Corps with very little idea of what they were doing. Gary Schaller was in his last year at South Dakota State College, studying agriculture and not knowing what to do next, when he got an informational letter from the Peace Corps. Not understanding what it was all about, he filled out a form and sent it in. Then he got a more detailed packet including an application, and again not really knowing what it was about he filled it out and sent it in. Finally, he got a letter saying he had been accepted for the Peace Corps in Nepal. When he asked his roommate if he'd ever heard of Nepal, like the others they had to get out a map to see where it was. He joined the Peace Corps group going to Nepal, knowing very little about either the Peace Corps or Nepal.

Richard Nishihara's case was similar. His high school in Maui, Hawaii, had held a school assembly marking the first anniversary of the Peace Corps, in which a Peace Corps film was shown. Afterwards a teacher went around the room asking for reactions, and everyone said it sounded great—different countries, adventurous opportunity, etc. As everyone was making a beeline for the door, the teacher grabbed Richard by the shoulder and said, "Why don't you apply?" Richard said, "Apply for what?" The Peace Corps, he was told. "Yeah, yeah, OK," was his response. A couple of days later the teacher handed Richard an application, which he filled out and mailed in, and then forgot about. About March he got a letter inviting him to join the Nepal group training program. He had no idea where Nepal was, but he was glad to go. He graduated from high school in Maui one day, and was on the plane for Washington the next.

Like Richard, Rich Emde was encouraged to apply before he had considered it an option. Rich was in his second year at Southern Illinois University and serving as the international affairs commissioner on the student council. One of his responsibilities was to make arrangements for a visiting Peace Corps recruiter. The recruiter asked Rich why he himself didn't apply, and Rich said he couldn't as he was only in his second year of college. The recruiter said that didn't matter, so Rich applied and was accepted for Nepal.

Similarly, John White was in his second year in Agricultural Sciences at Grambling College in Louisiana when he saw an advertisement for the Peace Corps. He and a friend thought, let's try it, we'll come back and finish college afterwards.

For some Volunteers, the Peace Corps offered less an alternative job, or an adventure, than a transition period after completing a degree. Jim and Franqui Scott were married seniors at Chico State in California, he in general agriculture and she in home economics, when they decided to join the Peace Corps "to have some time to adjust to life after college." They requested Borneo but were assigned to Nepal because of their academic backgrounds, which fit with what Nepal wanted.

These narratives of how people came to apply to the Peace Corps demonstrate the enormous number of different reasons and circumstances behind decisions to go to Nepal. For some there was an element of countercultural critique of modernity. We were all pre-baby boomer—albeit barely—

but we carried the seeds of restlessness that would later crystallize in the countercultural movements of the late 1960s and 1970s. For others, the opposite was the case: imbued with the benign, well-intentioned idea of bringing civilization, or progress, to poor parts of the world that needed it, theirs was more of a non-religious missionary impulse. For most of us, rather than some single compelling reason for joining the Peace Corps there was a mix of motivations behind our applications. If there is a common theme running throughout, it is that we were young and ready and eager for a change in our lives. All of us may have wanted different things, whether "answering Kennedy's call" or not, but we all wanted to do something different from what we were doing at the time, whatever that may have been.

Doing something different was also at least part of the motivation behind the three members of the group who were in their 40s or older: Dorothy Mierow, Les Richardson, and Lulu Miller. What differentiated them from the rest of us, almost all in our 20s, is that they had already lived much of their lives and actually done things, rather than merely contemplated what they might do. Whereas we were still in our starting blocks, they had already done a few laps.

Whatever the reasons and motivations, the application process, in retrospect, was often a comedy of errors: unintentional applications, conflicting offers to different countries (by telegram and letter), requests for Nepal met with offers elsewhere, requests for other countries that resulted in offers of Nepal, misinformation, lost telegrams and letters, and so on. If bureaucratic inefficiency was the price of being in on the ground floor of something fresh, innovative, and adventurous, we were happy to pay it.

Resistance to Volunteering

In addition to considering what motivated people to join, there was also the flip side—the strong resistance, in some cases, from parents and others who thought going into the Peace Corps was a terrible and misguided decision.

Mimi Smith's grandfather was a retired Marine Corps general, and he threatened to disinherit Mimi when she signed up for the Peace Corps. Her parents also were opposed to her joining the Peace Corps, but they eventually were mollified. Her grandfather was not. Lee Tuveson's father was skeptical of any kind of government employment and wanted Lee to get "a real job." Joyce Thorkelson's friends thought she would be doing nothing but digging ditches somewhere. Dan Pierce was finishing his B.A. in Physics at Stanford and feeling too burned out for graduate school right away. He applied for both Officer's Candidate School in the Navy, and the Peace Corps. He chose the Peace Corps, which upset his father greatly. In my own case, some friends of my parents were genuinely puzzled why anyone would join the Peace Corps, when, as one told me at a farewell party just before I left for Nepal, there was "good money to be made in dentistry." In retrospect, although I had no objections to good money, or having a good set of teeth, I don't think I ever had it in me to become a dentist.

There was also the hesitancy that led five to resign from the Peace Corps in the middle of training at George Washington University or Outward Bound. These resignations were prompted by personal reasons, such as romantic interests that would have to be put on hold for two years, or perhaps, according to the scuttlebutt, since such details were never articulated *per se*, the realization that the Peace Corps experience was just not for them. A more thorough account of Nepal I would include information about how not going to Nepal at all affected their lives, although that would be as impossible to determine as speculating on what would have happened to those who did go, had they not gone. We were all young, on the cusp of adulthood, and anything might have happened—more schooling, jobs of one sort or another, military service, marriage.

The narratives also underscore the profound changes in knowledge of international geography between the early 1960s and the second decade of the 21st century. Remote from most of the world's population centers, the population of America has long been ignorant of basic geographic facts about the world. As recently as 1988, 56% of Americans could not locate India on a map, and 11% of Americans could not even locate America on a map. It is therefore no surprise that in 1962 few of those selected to the first group of Peace Corps Volunteers would have heard of Nepal. In our general knowledge of the world, and in our travels to the rest of the world, we were no different from the population at large. In 1960 only 853,000 U.S. passports were issued; by 1970 that number had climbed to 2,219,000.[33] Volunteers in Nepal I played their part in contributing to that increase.

In the 21st century most Americans would still be hard pressed to locate Nepal on a map, but, by contrast, most would at least have heard of it, or at least have heard that there is a country with that name somewhere on the planet. A few would perhaps also know that Nepal is where Mt. Everest is. Fewer still would know that Nepal is where the Sherpas live, or where the Gurkha soldiers come from, or where Buddha was born. But with thousands of Returned Peace Corps Volunteers from Nepal scattered around the country over several decades, and many cable TV programs showing programs on environmental or mountaineering topics in the Himalayas, it's hard to imagine many in 21st century America confusing Nepal with Naples.

3

BECOMING NEPAL I

The Nepal I Group

Packing up the assorted paraphernalia accumulated after four years of college is not an activity I would want to repeat. But I somehow managed to compress it all into two suitcases and an attaché case, which, along with my portable typewriter (even in those pre-computer days I was pathologically dependent on a keyboard), I lugged onto the southbound train at Princeton Junction, the afternoon of June 13, one day after commencement. Arriving in Washington at 7:00 p.m. made me wonder if the Peace Corp would reprimand me, or even throw me out, for reporting two hours late. I needn't have worried. I wasn't even close to being the last of the 77 people to arrive at Hattie Strong Hall at George Washington University. Besides, at our briefing, which didn't begin till 8:00 p.m., I learned that I was assigned to teach in a university, not, as I had been previously informed, in a high school (I assumed this was a bureaucratic or clerical error), and that part of our training would be in Colorado, not Puerto Rico. It was difficult to avoid the impression that the program had been hastily thrown together, but that competent people were running the show and would handle whatever crises emerged from the organized chaos that seemed to be rampant.

After all the recruiting and applying and processing of applications, we were now going to enter the next stage of the process: learning how to live and work in Nepal. The Peace Corps distinguishes and keeps track of different groups of Volunteers in a country by numbering them in the order in which they arrive. That is how our group came to be called Nepal I, as opposed to later groups such as

Nepal II, Nepal III, and so on, up to Nepal 194, in 2004. The 77 of us took over, in its entirety, Strong Hall, which is still standing in downtown Washington, the site of all our sleeping and waking hours (including meals), class and training activities, and innumerable inoculations for every disease imaginable, regardless of the chances of our contracting it.

Among other surprises was a meeting the very next day with President Kennedy. We were shepherded over to the Chamber of Commerce Building where we heard from various Peace Corps officials, including Sargent Shriver, brother-in-law of the president and Peace Corps director, who gave an excellent, upbeat, and even inspiring talk. Finally, the President appeared on stage. After the wildly enthusiastic applause died down, he displayed the droll sense of humor for which he was famous, by saying, "I never expected to receive such a warm welcome from the Chamber of Commerce." He gave a well-received speech, and then took questions from the floor. We were a little shy about speaking up, but eventually someone asked if some day there might not be a domestic Peace Corps. He reacted to that suggestion positively (of course this was long before President Johnson's War on Poverty), and then dealt with a few more questions before departing. It's fair to say that the members of Nepal I were thrilled to see and hear the charismatic young president on their first full day in Washington. We were starting out at the top.

After that high moment life resumed at Strong Hall, where we rather quickly got to know each other. Mac Odell helped the process along with his antics. He met one person from California, another a little later and thought they should be introduced—only to find out they were a married couple. We didn't know anything about each other, but each residential floor (organized by gender) had to elect a representative to handle complaints and suggestions. Although I don't think anyone other than my roommate knew my name at that point, I was elected from my floor; Mac, irrepressible as ever, ran as a candidate from the girls' floor. If memory serves, his election bid failed.

Of the 77, five resigned for personal reasons sometime during the next three months, while two were "deselected" (see Training, below), leaving 70 Volunteers (55 men, 15 women) who would leave for Nepal that fall. Of the 70, nine left Nepal before the fulfillment of their two-year terms—seven for medical reasons, mostly pregnancies of married couples (even with relatively modern hospitals in Kathmandu, it was assumed that giving birth in Nepal was just too risky, although millions of Nepalese women seemed to manage it, as did my wife, who gave birth to our son eight years later). Two left in 1963 after barely half a year in Nepal, because of various personal difficulties experienced while attempting to adjust to living or working conditions in Nepal, which is a polite way of saying they were sent home. Both suffered from age-related difficulties, but of contrasting and instructive kinds: one, age 50, left because he was too old to adapt—to the food, the job, the language, and the Nepalis; the other, an 18-year-old fresh out of high school, left because, overwhelmed by the strangeness he encountered on all levels, he was too young to adapt.

Of the 70 who went to Nepal, eleven had died at the time of writing this book. Of the remaining 59, I was able to locate and interview all but eight. Of the eight, I couldn't find five, and three resisted discussing their Nepal experiences with me. A few of the others I did interview were initially hesitant to talk about those days, simply because they felt that the experience had been so intensely personal, profound, and life-defining that it did not bear scrutiny. Some of these latter Volunteers also provided the most detailed and thoughtful information, once they overcame their initial hesitation.

On the other hand, over the years after leaving Nepal the group had held four reunions: the 25th and 30th in Washington, D.C., the 38th in Nepal, and the 45th at my home in Northfield, MN, in addition to publishing four newsletters. Thus through these sources of information, plus the fact that I of course knew and had talked to everyone, especially before the diaspora from Nepal began, about some dimensions of their lives (place of origin, education, job in Nepal, etc.), I have at least some data on all 70. Another way to state this is that I have at least some information on everyone, and detailed information on many. Thus, the coverage is simultaneously complete and very uneven.

The characteristic of the group that is most central and also most difficult to convey is the closeness and bonding that for the most part Volunteers felt towards one another, even with our different interests and backgrounds. When we attended occasional conferences while working in Nepal, we were delighted to see each other. When Volunteers went trekking, whether on holiday or as part of an assignment, it was always a festive occasion to drop in on other Volunteers in their villages. Hospitality was just assumed; there was never any question that one would stay with whatever Volunteers happened to be living there. Mike Frame put it well in a letter home: "Here we depend very greatly on our few fellow Americans. We really share our troubles, our desires, our histories and expose our naked souls to each other, although had we been at home and met we probably would never even have had a serious conversation."[34] The frequency of reunions and newsletters attests to that continuing camaraderie. Volunteers who served in Nepal after our time there have told me that, oddly, some of the later Volunteer groups in Nepal experienced no such continuing sociability after returning home, and perhaps not even much while they were there. Perhaps being first provided an otherwise unattainable esprit.

Just before the 25th reunion of Nepal I, I attended my 25th college reunion. It was an enjoyable occasion at which I met and talked to and reminisced with old classmates—all the things I expected to do and was expected to do at a major college reunion. But the 25th Nepal I reunion a few days later was an event of an entirely different character. Even though, as at the college reunion, few of us had seen each other during the preceding 25 years, at the Peace Corps reunion there was an overpowering venting of emotion just to be together again, showing our slides of Nepal and swapping tall tales. It was much more like a family reunion (without the usual tensions) than anything else.

Perhaps the feeling of closeness is best expressed by Les Gile in a letter he wrote to "Peace Corps Friends" in October, 2008:

"It was at the west end of Pokhara valley looking up the road to Tansen, where I began my first solo journey in Nepal, with fear. I was journeying to see Peace Corps friends teaching in Tansen—Jane Stevens, Ken Martin, Bill Clayton, and Joann Marchand, if I remember correctly. It was an interesting trip. Slept with bedbugs and mangy dogs, got carried over the river by young Nepalese Gurung soldier recruits on the other side of the river. I shared my tangerines with them, stepped over dead animal bodies, and crossed expansive rivers.

I have those same fears now as my second bout with terminal cancer begins, far advanced lung, liver, trachea, hip, stomach, and brain. I do not know how long I have, but wanted to tell you that I have loved and cared deeply for each of you and feel very blessed by your friendships. I have had a very rich life and you were part of it!"

My best guess is that most of us reciprocated the sentiments that Les expressed in his letter, and with the same intensity. Les died a few days after writing it, on October 20, 2008.

Race and Ethnicity

In Chapter One I referred to the diversity ("racially, ethnically, religiously, educationally, and economically") of Nepal I. That is only half the story, however, since I might just as easily characterize the homogeneity of the group.

Racially, as that term is used in absurdly inaccurate, unscientific, and folk (but popular) American discourse, the group was white except for four African Americans and one Japanese American. Ethnically and religiously it also was overwhelmingly white middle American. All were of Christian—whether Catholic or Protestant—background, whether they were currently believers and practitioners or not. Four grew up speaking European languages, and three were recent European immigrants whose citizenship was hurried along so that they could join the Peace Corps, but all spoke colloquial, unaccented English. The closest anyone came to being Jewish is one man (who was president of his local atheist society) whose mother was a Russian Jew; similarly, Nishihara had one Japanese parent. There were no other Asian Americans, while Hispanics, Native Americans, Hindus, Buddhists and Muslims were entirely lacking in the group.

Given the general bonhomie that characterized relations among the members of Nepal I, I believe all the white members of the group would be as astonished as I was to learn that one of the four African Americans was quite sensitive to what he felt was an inherent, implicit, if low-level racism on the part of the white members of the group towards him. As far as I am aware, none of the whites were consciously aware of race as an issue, and the bulk of the civil rights movement was yet to come. We did not immediately know, given the general lack of American news, about the big civil rights events that took place while we were in Nepal, such as James Meredith's enrolling as the first African American at the University of Mississippi, the murder of Medgar Evers, and the elimination of the poll tax. We certainly were unaware that the Crayola Crayon Company renamed its "Flesh" crayon "Peach" in 1962.[35] According to the other three African Americans in the group, they tried to convince the fourth that he was among friends and supporters, but he retained what they said they regarded as a chip on his shoulder. He never revealed or even hinted at the existence of his feelings to the majority whites. He went on to a lengthy and successful career with USAID, in Vietnam, and with the State Department. Unfortunately, he was one of the five I failed to locate.

On the other hand, Carl Jorgensen, one of the other three African Americans, had what in many ways was a polar opposite experience. He commented, "You know, Arthur Ashe, the great tennis player who lived a very integrated life, once said, 'I'm reminded I'm black every hour of my life.' I would say that was true for me too except for the time that I was in Nepal. Because in Nepal, the Nepalis really didn't care that much. I mean, I was to them primarily an American. The Americans were fairly liberal, but in the States, if a white person had a friendship with a black person, they had a price to pay for it. In Nepal in 1962, they didn't." What made the two years spent with Nepal I so special is that it was the first time in his life he felt he didn't live in a racialized environment—among either Nepalis or white Americans. Thus Carl and the wary African American mentioned above represent contrary extremes of minority reaction to the white majority of Nepal I. Generalizations about race are therefore impossible to frame.

Perhaps John White's experience is more revealing than either of the opposite poles mentioned above. Although an African American, his sentiments were not couched in racial terms at all. Even more positively than Carl, he describes how empowering the whole Peace Corps experience was for him. He said that being in the Peace Corps made him realize how fortunate he was to have the freedom to do what he wanted. "Freedom to go to school, to go into business, freedom to do what I want in life. I think that opened my eyes to how fortunate we are. When I came back my perspective on life was totally changed. Everything I did was positive. I had no problem with things in college, I had no problem with my jobs. During that time I bought a 30 acre ranch in Texas because in America you can do what you want to. I just had a great zest for life after I came back."

Educationally, the overwhelming majority had some college experience: out of the 70, seven held master's degrees, 46 had B.A.'s, and another 19 had had a few years of college. Five had completed high school only. One older man had not finished high school, but had received diplomas in welding, cooking, and baking. None of the Volunteers had Ph.D.'s, but the senior resident staff did. Representative Bates held a Ph.D. in English, while Deputy Representative Unsoeld had received a Ph.D. in philosophy.

About 20 were from predominantly rural or farming backgrounds, 50 from towns or cities. Economically most were of middle class or lower middle class origin, with a small sprinkling from the upper middle class. It's hard to know exactly since the term "class" has no clear empirical referent, and even if it did, in American society the details of class background are discussed or disclosed less candidly than even those of sexual behavior.[36] I'm aware of only three known gays/lesbians in the group, although none were "out" at the time. My intuitive guess is that there may have been five or six gays/lesbians (some of them bi-) in Nepal I.

While in many ways most members of the group felt themselves to be fairly "typical" young Americans, this is partly because in those days ethnic, religious, "racial" or age-based minorities were not marked categories. That is, they existed, but they were not much remarked upon, singled out, or thought about by the majority white society, except in mostly pejorative ways. They were certainly marked for individuals in those groups.

But there were sociological pockets of the country quite unrepresented in the Peace Corps, at least in the beginning or at least in this particular group of Volunteers. Where were the Jews, East Asians, Hispanics, Asian Americans (other than Nishihara), Native Americans, and other minorities in the Peace Corps? Even the proportion of African Americans in Nepal I was less than half that of the population at large. The Peace Corps, like the government and the rest of the society more generally in those times, was largely a project of middle-class Protestant-Catholic Americans of European origin. While others were certainly welcome to the Peace Corps and even urged to apply to it, with so few of their own kind involved they may have felt less motivated to join in the fun. They were busy enough trying to consolidate their credentials, if they had them, or to "make it" financially in mainstream society, if they didn't, and the Peace Corps could not help in either case.

This phenomenon was true not only for the Peace Corps. When the Chinese American Julia Chang Bloch became ambassador to Nepal in 1989, she was the first Asian American ambassador in the history of the American Foreign Service. No doubt many Asian Americans had the educational, social, political, and financial credentials to serve as an ambassador before her, but, given the subtle bias and racism coursing through the body politic, they had little choice but to cultivate and strengthen those hard-won credentials, rather than enter public service, at least in the international sphere. To a lesser extent, the same may have been true of Jews. This was a time when, by social and cultural default, positions of power and influence tended to go to WASPs—not until Henry Kissinger came along in 1973 had a Jew been appointed Secretary of State. Even Catholics labored under suspicions from the Protestant majority. President Kennedy's electoral success in 1960 was considered a major breakthrough for Catholic politicians. By the 21st century Catholic or Protestant identity of presidential candidates had become irrelevant and often even unknown.

For Blacks, the situation was quite different. Being excluded from mainstream society and embargoed from its economic wherewithal and political clout had been the lot of African Americans for centuries. It would not be surprising if they therefore were not inclined, at least initially, to think that the Peace Corps would be any different. After all, racial integration of the armed forces had taken place only in 1948, Brown vs. Board of Education was settled in 1954, and Rosa Parks refused to move to the back of the bus in Montgomery, Alabama, in 1955, only six years before the Peace Corps was established. The civil rights movement was still young, and the Freedom Rides to Mississippi took place just months before our training began. It would take a little time to become clear that the Peace Corps, its explicit idealistic underpinnings notwithstanding, was ideologically several steps ahead of standard government bureaucracies of the times.

Put another way, the needs the Peace Corps met in those who applied were perhaps not felt by those who stayed away. The latter were more interested either in breaking into mainstream American life for the first time (Blacks, Hispanics), or securing their hard-won place in it (Jews, Asians), while the former (mainstream Whites, which is what we mostly were) were trying either to reform American society or to break away from it. The Peace Corps provided

those from poorer backgrounds the wherewithal to see parts
of the planet they increasingly were learning about from
the still new and ever-widening world of television. Those
from the middle and upper middle classes wanted a change
from what had become for them the stale and uninspiring
traditions of establishment, 1950s America.

Another reason that diversity, or the lack of it, was not
much noticed in the group is that we were all very busily
and intensely focused on just one goal: going to Nepal.
Everything we did, from dawn to dusk, was aimed in that
direction: language classes, area studies classes, job-oriented
classes, American studies classes, health studies classes. No
one had the time or energy or even interest to investigate
each other's backgrounds, because they just didn't seem
relevant to the task at hand. We were obsessed with Nepal,
which trumped not only personal background, but all other
activities and interests.

This is not to say that friendships and mini-groups didn't
form, since of course they did, as they would in any group
of that size. There was a natural tendency for those with
more or less education to associate with each other, or those
with farming backgrounds to seek each other out. But these
smaller groupings were submerged in the more embracing,
we're-all-going-to-Nepal identity.

The four African Americans didn't form a clique unto
themselves, although they could hardly help recognizing
commonalities. As noted above, they had very different
reactions to being part of the overwhelmingly white
group—from being relieved at being totally accepted to
being chronically suspicious of possible, if only imagined,
slights. Different religious or ethnic origins among whites
were either unknown or, where known, ignored.

Another way to put all this is to say that for almost all
of us, regardless of our personal life histories, life started
anew at George Washington University. Apart from the
usual and superficial "Where're you from?" questions that
Americans ask when they meet strangers, no one had much
interest, and certainly not enough time, to delve much into
each other's personal histories or backgrounds. What might

happen in the future overwhelmed what had happened, or might have happened, in the past.

To the extent that none of us knew anything about Nepal, which was mostly true, we were all on a level playing field. Class, race, education, and place of origin did not privilege anyone with regard to knowledge of Nepal. Our world was Nepal-driven, and any topic not relevant to that world tended to be shoved onto conversational backburners.

Staff

In an official, bureaucratic sense, the group referred to as Nepal I consisted of the Volunteers whom history offered up to it. But in another, looser, and more social and almost spiritual sense, the administrative staff in the Kathmandu office was also part of the group.

As noted above, Bob Bates[37] was Representative, or the Peace Corps Rep, as he was informally called. He was not only a distinguished educator, but he also had a reputation as one of the most accomplished American explorers/ mountaineers of his generation. He was most famous as a member of the American expedition to K2 in 1953, which was caught in a brutal storm near the summit and came very close to perishing (Bob had also been on K-2 in 1938). In addition, he had a history of exploration in the Arctic, and in the 1930s he made the third ascent of Denali, at 20,320 ft. the highest peak on the North American continent.

Bob's deputy, Willi Unsoeld,[38] was a noted mountaineer of the next generation, whose fame increased after he led the first ascent of Mt. Everest via the West Ridge in 1963 (Peace Corps gave him a leave of absence to do this while he was Deputy Representative), and then traversed the peak and descended it via the southeast ridge route which Sir Edmund Hillary and Tenzing Norgay had pioneered in 1953. Willi was a charismatic raconteur who could spellbind Volunteers with tales of his adventures, from the first ascent of Masherbrum, in the Karakorum, to climbing in the Cascade mountains of

Washington with only one half of a pair of crampons simply because he couldn't find the other half for his other foot.

Both Bob and Willi, and their families, had gone through the training program with the Volunteers in Washington, which made their membership in Nepal I seem even more natural. Since they ate with us and sat in on all our classes, it was difficult to think of them as anything other than part of our group. In Nepal, they took us in when we were sick and needed to recuperate from this or that illness, usually intestinal. They also advised us as we negotiated this or that personal crisis, whether in Nepal or involving plans or relationships stateside, stretched and sometimes twisted out of shape by communication difficulties (mail took weeks, and for all practical purposes there was no phone service between the two countries). This web of support would not have existed without the warm and nurturing presence of Gail Bates and Jolene Unsoeld.

Since Bob Bates had been given only a year's leave from Exeter, Willi was poised to follow him as the next Representative. However, when Willi was hospitalized for months in Kathmandu for the frostbite he suffered during a bivouac above 28,000 ft. on Everest, he was temporarily replaced by Bill Warren. Bill was transferred from the Peace Corps office in the Philippines, where he had been deployed in the first year of the Peace Corps there. As much as anyone, Bill embodied the enthusiasm and idealism of the Peace Corps. During our second year, with Bates and Unsoeld gone (Willi had been evacuated to the U.S. after contracting hepatitis in Shanta Bhawan, the Kathmandu hospital, while being treated for his frostbitten toes), Bill, although an "outsider" to us and to Nepal, quickly became socialized, along with his wife, Jay, into the larger Nepal I group.

Each of us knew and were closer to some staff than we were to others, depending on where we were stationed, what our job was, and the vagaries of personal chemistry. What stood out for all of us in spite of these minor and idiosyncratic interpersonal differences was that all these initial Peace Corps staff afforded us such great respect, affection, latitude, and support in what we were trying to accomplish. When we needed them they were there, and when we didn't, they kept a respectful distance.

Finally, the Nepali staff was headed by a remarkable man named Dhruba Bhakta. Dhruba came from a family which had been active in overthrowing, in 1950, the despotic Rana regime that had ruled Nepal since 1846. In 1941 the Ranas had executed Dhruba's brother, Dharma Bhakta, one of the "Four Martyrs" who had fought against them, and whose statues stand in the Tundkikhel parade ground in Kathmandu today. As a vigorous opponent of the Rana regime, Dhruba had to live for years in the Indian towns of Darjeeling and Kalimpong, just over the border, where he helped raise money from traders in Tibet to support the fight against the Ranas. Once the Ranas were overthrown, he returned to Nepal, where he worked for USAID and then the Peace Corps.

Dhruba handled much of the office work that needed to be processed. Even an organization as avowedly anti-bureaucratic as the Peace Corps generated its share of paper (especially in pre-email and pre-internet times), in traffic back to Washington as well as to and from various ministries of the government of Nepal. Dhruba also provided real glue with his continuity, as American staff came and went through the revolving door. For some he became a father figure, as when he played the role of father of the bride for one of the Volunteer marriages. With almost no exceptions, Dhruba, Bob, Willi, and Bill were older than we were, and we were happy to seek and relieved to receive their wisdom and counsel when we needed it.

An example of that avuncular advising is contained in a letter Unsoeld wrote from his hospital bed in September, 1963, when he wasn't preoccupied with watching nine of his ten toes, blackened by frostbite, fall off. We received his letter when we had finished our first year in country and were halfway through our two-year stint:

"We members of Nepal I have spent just short of a year on the job now and are clearly ripe for all sorts of reactions. In many cases the first flush of novelty has long since worn off and been replaced by a sense of those harsh and disappointing facts which seem to control life and to slow progress in Nepal. Agriculture students appear no more eager to pitch in and do manual work than they did eleven months ago, SLC [School Leaving Certificate, the equivalent of a high school diploma] exams and teaching methods seem just as ill-adjusted to the realities of modern life, faculties and School Committees seem just as unmotivated, students seem just as dishonest, and life for the PCV has turned out often to be just plain dull. In addition to these frustrations, there has also been added recently the sense of being neglected by the PC staff—a feeling of being allowed to drift aimlessly with no firm hand at the helm. With Dr. Bates counting on leaving soon and with me counting my toes, also leaving soon, staff confusion in the past few months has been admittedly considerable.

However, against this somber background I would like to sketch in a few administrative attitudes and principles which will greatly help to guide our relationships during our remaining time together in Nepal.

First of all, it is my firm conviction that nine months should be considered ample time in which to make a solid contribution to PC aims in Nepal. It is all too easy to feel that if your towering personal triumph has not come off in the first eleven months, then another ten will surely be inadequate. Such is simply not the case. Despite the set of some Volunteers towards simply hanging on until the bitter end it is my conviction that the final ten months of our project can prove to be far more rewarding than was the first half. After all, you will know your jobs better, know the Nepalis better, and be known by them better.

Naturally this greater mutual knowledge will often result in violent rearrangements of some of your earlier hopes and ambitions. Some of you will have already found that the local situation is not advanced enough to benefit fully from your talents. Others will have found your talents not advanced enough for the local situation. In both cases better compromises should be possible in the light of your greater mutual knowledge. And in neither case should the lack of technical productivity have any fatal effect on the other two PC objectives of knowing and being known by the local Nepalis.

I do not expect any startling breakthroughs in the next ten months in your technical contributions to Nepalese education or agriculture. The direction and extent of such contributions should be pretty well established by now. But in the realm of getting to know your Nepali acquaintances— of deepening your knowledge and appreciation of their ways of doing (and not doing), of thinking, of feeling, living, and dying—here I see the possibility for amazing advances in our last ten months. Technical contributions are limited by your experience and training, but the establishment of mutual understanding depends ultimately upon your qualities as a human being."

Willi had perspicaciously noticed that we were almost exactly half way through our tour, when the initial rush of enthusiasm had worn off, doubts had developed about whether we were accomplishing anything, and we couldn't quite see the light at the end of the tunnel. His letter was obviously intended to perk up our occasionally flagging spirits.

These people—Bob, Willi, and Bill, and their families, plus Dr. Mark Rhine and his wife, Claire—were not Volunteers. They were paid government salaries and lived in housing provided with most of the amenities usually available in the United States (but not television, which would not exist in Nepal for another 20 years). Although they were not Volunteers, they were perceived as possessing a spiritual affinity with the Volunteers of Nepal I.

They were followed by several generations of American staff over the years, some temporary, some longer term. Some were cut from the same mold of bureaucratic procedures and mindsets as civil servants who could be found in any federal government office. More disappointingly, some of the American staff in subsequent years were political appointees, vetted at high government levels for a proven record of loyalty, in those times of anti-war and pro-civil rights rebellion, to the Republican Party. But there was no hint of that the first year or two, when idealism, enthusiasm, energy, and leadership skills (acquired from mountaineering for Bob and Willi, and from Peace Corps experience in the Philippines for Bill) were all that were required to be appointed to a Peace Corps staff position, whether overseas or in Washington.

Training

The prevailing wisdom in the early years of the Peace Corps was that in order to survive and thrive for two years in Nepal, three months of training in the United States were required. This would enable Volunteers to acquire job skills, language facility, and general familiarity with what the Peace Corps experience would be like. The concern was that no one be sent overseas until thoroughly vetted, to avoid embarrassing mistakes during the start-up time when Peace Corps was still subject to criticism as a foolish, idealistic venture, and its Volunteers too young and inexperienced to sustain existence and succeed in these distant, difficult countries. Stateside training was very costly, however, so after a few years caution was thrown to the winds and all that training was done, at much less expense, "in country."

George Washington University

For program components such as American studies, health, and job-related training, the staff of George Washington University was hired to give lectures and conduct classes over a two-month period. For Nepali language, the university hired a Washington area polymath, Randolph Carr, with experience in the State Department and in language teaching, to develop and supervise a program of instruction. Four Nepali employees at the U.S. Embassy and USAID (one from the former, three from the latter) in Nepal were brought over as native-speaker instructors, to join three Nepali students in the U.S. on summer vacation, and two daughters of the Nepalese Ambassador, M. P. Koirala, who helped out from time to time. Since no established program of Nepali language instruction was then available, class materials were prepared one day—usually less—ahead of the time they were needed. If Carr's thermofax machine had malfunctioned (the age of Xerox was not yet upon us), the Nepali language program would have collapsed.

Classes had to fit the needs of a wide variety of academic backgrounds. Five had not gone beyond high school, including one who had not graduated from high school. Even among the college graduates there was a range between agriculture graduates from large state universities and liberal arts students from mostly smaller private colleges. Although the group acquired a certain homogeneity because of its common experiences, goals, and destination, those from less privileged educational backgrounds initially felt a little in awe of some of those with more education, or at least what was perceived as more elite (e.g., Ivy League) education. Those perceived differences disappeared rather rapidly, as the less educated came to see that we all had feet of clay, and the more educated began to see and admire the skills and practical knowledge that they lacked and that the less formally educated possessed.

Learning was not confined to the classroom. In the dorm rooms and at the cafeteria we got to know each other, our foibles and idiosyncrasies. One evening I met one of our older members at the water fountain in a dormitory hallway. He had just taken a drink and commented that the water "don't agree with me none." I thought immediately that if he didn't like the water coming out of a cooler in Washington, how would he take to the food in Nepal? Not very well, it turned out, and he had to leave Nepal early.

There was another somewhat muted, but pervasive and consequential, component of the training program. The Peace Corps faced considerable skepticism, and even hostility, from some conservative members of Congress and the press and in the country at large. Therefore the Peace Corps went to great lengths to be sure Volunteers had the right stuff—that they would perform well and not do anything that might cast the new Kennedy government in Washington in a bad light. Batteries of psychological tests were given to trainees, and conduct in all aspects of training was carefully, if covertly, monitored by teachers and staff. Being under constant surveillance placed all trainees under considerable stress and worry that they might be "deselected."

In the event, only two were deselected (a married couple who had difficulty making up their minds whether this was something they really wanted to do or not), while five resigned for personal reasons. But the possibility of deselection hovered over the entire training process, lending it a threatening air of ambiguity, uncertainty, and fear.

Reviews of the George Washington training program by Volunteers were mixed. Most trainees either liked the training program, or liked most parts of it while disliking other parts. In the latter case, training was seen simply as a necessary evil that would be blessedly brief, at least compared to the longer-term, great adventure that awaited us in Nepal. Overall, training had something for everyone, but not everyone felt that everything was worthwhile.

On the negative side, Al Champney complained that eleven hours of class/day allowed no time to study. This meant that the training staff tried to do more than they could achieve, and so were unsuccessful. While our ignorance of Nepal mostly placed us all on the same level, the occasional high-level lecture was inappropriate for those who had never attended college.

The most compelling critique of training was not evident until Volunteers were on the job in Nepal. We were all sent to Nepal to work at some kind of job, yet, incongruously, job training was virtually non-existent. Despite the fact that most Volunteers would be teachers in Nepal, and that few had any prior experience teaching, there was no preparation— for example, practice-teaching—at George Washington that would help Volunteers on that first day when they walked into a Nepali classroom. We learned facts about Nepalese education (literacy rates, or attitudes towards learning, for example), but we were not taught, as future educators, how to deal with such facts on a practical, day-to-day level.

On the other hand, many Trainees found the training

experience to be fun and exciting, partly because it introduced them for the first time to east-coast urban life. Some of us used to run up and down the Washington monument in our free time, just to work off extra energy. Bob Murphy thought that just living and studying in Washington was enough. He discovered rules and regulations new to him. He went to a bar not far from our training site, where the bartender yelled at him when he got up with a beer in his hand to go to another table (to talk to some girls there), because it was illegal to stand up in a bar with a drink in hand. None of us knew why—perhaps it was similar to the law against having an open beer bottle in a moving car. As for the classes, he found them exciting because they were being designed as we went along. In the case of language classes this led to spontaneity; one of the Nepali instructors, Shiva Rai, taught trainees many of the more common swear words in Nepali.

When Bob Rhoades discovered he was going to Nepal instead of Italy, he became more interested in the whole experience. Meeting other trainees in Washington was his first encounter with people from different walks of life, who spoke with different accents—from his limited social background in rural Oklahoma, he was suddenly exposed to many new things. For him, that was the merit of going through the training program.

For Gary Schaller, too, it was the first time he had rubbed shoulders with people who had gone to colleges like Harvard, Yale, Princeton, and Dartmouth, as well as people from California. As a Midwestern farm kid he felt a little out of place at first. But he had a good time, getting to know other people and learning to get along with them.

Trainees were also given full medical and dental exams while they were in Washington. Bob Shrader, from rural West Virginia, had never in his life been to a dentist. All his teeth were rotted out inside the enamel rims, so he acquired a whole set of tooth fillings during training. What we were not told, however, is that we were all guinea pigs for dental students who needed the practice, regardless of the need for treatment. When they tried to remove all my perfectly good fillings and replace them, I simply refused their services and produced a letter from my dentist in Kentucky to the effect that my teeth were fine the way they were. Another example of incompetence was our class in first aid, in which the instructor, asked what the normal human pulse is, answered 42 (the true range is 60-80). We often thought that language training was not the only part of training that was thrown together at the last minute.

For John White, the training program was an eye-opener to a whole new world. Flying to Washington from Louisiana was the first time John had ever been on an airplane. Indeed, for several Trainees, traveling to Washington was their first airplane ride.

On the whole I enjoyed the time at George Washington, not so much for its substance as for the process of getting to know 69 people, none of whom came from my part of the country, and only a few of whom had a background much like mine, so novelties were almost endless and, to me, fascinating. I looked down my nose at some of the classes, most conspicuously at a two-hour lecture by the chairman (the title of "Chair" did not exist then) of the physical education department, whose main message, about physical hygiene, was that in Nepal we should be sure to wash our hands before eating and brush our teeth. It was so childish that it took a moment for me to realize that he was serious. Unfortunately I have never been very good at concealing the contempt I feel for ineptitude or stupidity. It still gets me into trouble, although in this case the teacher was too occupied with his hygiene rules to notice that I had an attitude.

I had no such feelings of contempt in language class. Like everyone else, upon arrival in Washington I didn't know a word of Nepali. I still remember the thrill of learning my first word: "pyaz" (onion), and I entertained the absurd ambition to learn all the words in Nepali. To this day I am constantly learning new words, and they seem as endless to me now as they did then. During one class Mr. Carr asked me to come teach another language section for a few minutes. I was terrified at the prospect, but I had to suppose it meant that I was doing all right. At the end of the program we had a little commencement exercise, and I was asked to give an oration in Nepali. I worked quite hard on it, and the audience seemed to catch all of my jokes. One of my lines played on our frustration and discomfort with all the dental work we were required to undergo. I said, "Unfortunately, we all have teeth", and since we hadn't learned the word for teeth yet, I had to bare my gums while saying the word "dant", hoping that they would catch the connection to the cognate "dental", which of course they did.

Washington was a delightful and exciting place to spend the summer, but not a very good venue to serve as a stepping stone to the rigors of life in Nepal. To provide both spice and relief from the rigidities of training, we welcomed distractions such as the following: a stroll along the C&O canal with Justice William Douglass (who was trying to preserve it as a landmark); the ambassadors from Nepal to the U.S. and from the U.S. to Nepal, who spoke to us; the occasional visit from the Peace Corps director, Sargent Shriver; private parties on weekends with friends and family of various trainees who lived in the area; the existence of Bromley's Bar a couple of blocks away, a pleasant source of cold beer after a long hot day of classes (and compensation for the total lack of any Indian restaurants in Washington at that time).

Finally, we had two meetings with President Kennedy, the first (with several hundred other Trainees in the Washington area) at the U.S. Chamber of Commerce (described above), and the second on the south lawn of the White House (again with several hundred other Trainees). At the White House the president spoke briefly about the importance of the Peace Corps and then read off a list describing the jobs of each group (and asking them to raise their hands so he could recognize them) and which country they would be working in. The main interest and attraction of the event was simply being on the White House grounds and up as close as we wanted to be with the president. Although in hindsight this should have loomed as a big moment, at the time I was a recent college graduate and a philosophy major, and I thought I knew it all. My cast of mind was to be somewhat suspicious and even cynical about most things. Moreover, the hero worship of Kennedy that persists to this day (despite all the character flaws that have been documented *ad nauseum*) wasn't as strong then as it became in the years following his assassination. I'm a good example: I would say that I'm more impressed by him now (given the presidents we've suffered through since JFK) than I was then.

Outward Bound

The second phase of our training, at Outward Bound in Colorado (near Marble CO, population 5) provided a sharp contrast from all these urban amenities, and a welcome change for those who loved the mountains (not so for those who didn't). The basic philosophy of Outward Bound is that by pushing people to extremes, to levels beyond their normal capacities, way beyond their comfort zones, they build the strength and self-reliance to do more than they think they can. This is one component of the more comprehensive Outward Bound outlook encapsulated, officially, in the motto, "To serve, to strive, and not to yield"[39]—words which either inspired or annoyed us when we heard them repeatedly at Outward Bound.

Not everyone bought the idea of pushing to physical limits, which took such forms as early morning runs (including dashing through a cold stream) and learning mountaineering techniques (including rappelling, belaying, and crossing rope bridges). But the big events were the hikes, some lasting several days, such as the "solo survival" hike during which we were supposed to live off the land for three days, by finding berries or killing frogs. Despite good intentions, I never did bring myself to kill and clean the couple of dozen tree frogs which would have made a meal. If I was overweight before that hike, I wasn't afterwards. But the biggest hike was the final one of about 50 miles, involving glissading down glaciers and bushwhacking when the trails ended.

Al Champney thought the fact that both Nepal and Colorado were mountainous was irrelevant, and the

Outward Bound experience had nothing to do with our assignments. He also thought that the mountain training was detrimental to language training, which more or less ground to a halt in Colorado.

Similarly, Beverly Fogg thought, "some of the training was unbelievably stupid. In Colorado, women lived in tents in one end of the camp, with men in the other end. Even married couples were separated." In her view, the fact that one of the wives wanted to show that the women could out-walk, out-climb, and outlast the men showed how silly the whole Outward Bound mystique was. In those pre-gender equality days no one worried about such things; I never discovered whether the wife in question was successful or not.

The character of the Outward Bound training was dramatically different from that at George Washington University because of a strong and omnipresent finger-wagging morality that was being preached in the cool Colorado air. Outward Bound was designed for younger groups of junior high and high school urban kids who had never experienced nature in the raw. In the mostly college-educated Nepal I group, the average age was several years older than that of the usual Outward Bound clientele, and those extra years made a tremendous difference in how we reacted to their moralistic pedagogy. So when they gave us junior high or high school rules to follow (no smoking, for example, long before the anti-smoking movement), we thought they must be kidding.

Beverly, a smoker, cheated and smoked surreptitiously. At the end of the training, when it came time to receive her Outward Bound certificate, she told them that she could not accept it in good conscience, because she had smoked. They told her to take it anyway, to which she replied that that would be hypocritical.

I pursued an opposite strategy. I announced at the beginning that I did not smoke, and even if I did, I did not intend to smoke at Outward Bound, but for me this was a personal matter beyond the purview of Outward Bound. I therefore refused to sign the pledge that I would not smoke, and thus did not receive the Outward Bound certificate; they did not even offer me the option of keeping it anyway.

Carl Jorgensen also found the Outward Bound experience exasperating, but for a different reason. He said the gung-ho orientation of Outward Bound drove him crazy. When the Outward Bound staff said, "This is the most important thing you'll ever do—or hardest thing you'll ever do," Carl thought, "I'm black, and how in the hell can this be the hardest thing I'll ever do?" But he knew he couldn't tell the Outward Bound staff that.

Joyce Thorkelson enjoyed both Washington and Colorado, although she and her tent-mate, Helen Carter, tried hard to get out of the morning run, where you had to run, jump in a creek, and then run some more. They would lag at the back of the pack so they wouldn't have to jump in the creek.

Unlike some others, Mimi Smith was grateful for the intensity and difficulty she had to face at Outward Bound. She felt the resilience she acquired going through all those physically difficult activities helped her confront the difficult physical situations she later faced in her village, Dhankuta, in east Nepal. The first time she trekked there it took her almost two days to complete the hike from Dharan, but two years later she could make it all the way in a single day.

FBI Clearance

Trainees also had to go through a process of security clearance before being cleared to go to Nepal. This involved a so-called full field investigation by the FBI. The process involved FBI agents who visited any and all places trainees had lived and studied during the several years prior to the training period. They conducted door-to-door interviews with neighbors and colleagues in an attempt to uncover any unsavory characteristics in a trainee's background that might adversely affect performance in Nepal. All Volunteers eventually passed muster, but the arrival of a few of them in Nepal was delayed until these protracted investigations could be finished.

At the conclusion of training Doug Bingham and Mac Odell were told their background reports had problems. They could only wonder: had they been spotted in a political demonstration, hung out with the wrong kids in college, taken courses from a "leftist" professor? Anxious and concerned, they could only sit around and speculate till the clearances came through. They headed for Nepal right away to join the rest of the group there. They never knew what the problem was and soon forgot all about it.

Years later some family friends asked Mac's parents if Mac had had any more problems with the FBI. It turns out they had been approached by an FBI agent who asked lots of questions, to which the friends had given lots of unequivocally positive answers. Then a few weeks later a second agent came asking similar questions. Being suspicious, this time the friends refused to cooperate. Finally the second agent relented and told them what had happened. After questioning many people, the original agent had returned to his hotel, where he keeled over from a fatal heart attack before writing up his notes. A second agent was finally recruited to conduct the background check all over again, resulting in the belated clearances.

The investigations were supposed to be confidential, but sometimes they were not. One day Bob Murphy was mowing the lawn in front of his house in Oakland, CA. An FBI agent came along, introduced himself, and said he'd like to ask him some questions about Robert Murphy. The agent didn't ask the name of the person he was interviewing. So he asked Bob what kind of person Murphy was, and Bob told him. At the end of his questioning, he asked Bob his name, for the record. Bob told him he'd been speaking to the individual he'd been asking about. The agent was pretty upset and said Bob shouldn't have withheld that information. But the agent went off and talked to neighbors, who immediately called Bob and told him all the good things they'd said about him.

Bob felt that this FBI clearance procedure was only part of the process that got him started in his new life. He felt that the Peace Corps was a crack in the door opening out onto the wider world, and that he had just stepped through it.

It seems the FBI is always with us. Later, in about 1968, Bob Murphy was contacted again, this time when Bob Proctor's background was being checked for State Department clearance. He gave Proctor a rosy recommendation. About the same period Proctor was contacted by another investigator looking into Murphy's background, and he gave him a comparably glowing recommendation. They each got the jobs that had triggered the FBI investigations. They report becoming inseparable friends ever after, having come to know deeply and personally the rewards of scratching one another's backs.

4

AMERICANS GLOBALIZING
AND GLOBALIZED

Getting There

Of all the difficulties we had been told to expect during training, simply getting to Nepal in the first place was a challenge we had not anticipated. Assembling in early September in New York for a numbingly long, propeller-driven Pan Am charter flight to Delhi, dipping down to refuel in London and Beirut, was easy enough. After the Outward Bound mountain training had ceremoniously concluded (with awarding of certificates to some, but not to me, because of my refusal to sign the no-smoking pledge, or to Beverly, because she confessed to cheating), we had been given a week or so of home leave to say final good-byes and pack up, so we were ready to go.

The main problem was the weather. The first morning in Delhi a few of us got up at 3:00 a.m. to go to the airport for our onward flight to Kathmandu (the twin-engine DC-3 could not begin to hold all of us, so we were split into several groups to fly over a period of several days). But lingering monsoon rains in the Himalayas forced postponement of our flight. Going overland was not possible because of flooding in the Gangetic plain and political instability along the border.

Less than two years before our arrival, in December 1960, in a surprise move King Mahendra had jailed the first democratically elected Prime Minister, B. P. Koirala, and all of his cabinet. His followers in the Congress Party had shown their defiance of the King by staging rebellious acts from their safe havens just over the border in India. Counter attacks followed by the armed forces of Nepal, making it difficult for foreigners to get into (or out of) Nepal by an overland route.

Since we were going to Nepal by invitation of HMG (His Majesty's Government), we had been told relatively little of this background political intrigue. But we did know that most of Nepal was difficult to reach because of the lack of roads in the mountains. Still, we had not realized that even getting into the country was going to be such a logistical challenge. During the summer, while we were in training, two planes had crashed in the mountains of Nepal, wiping out half of the Royal Nepal Airlines Corporation fleet. The unintended delay of several days gave us the unanticipated opportunity, until the weather cleared, to tour Delhi, see nearby sites such as the Taj Mahal, and visit the American Embassy for a welcome from Ambassador John Kenneth Galbraith.

While we were waiting at our hotel, the Oberoi Swiss, for our flights to Kathmandu, Bob Proctor borrowed one of the bearer's outfits to wear out "on the town," so as not to be recognized, he thought, as a foreigner. "After generating more stares than anonymity, I retreated back to the hotel, floppy turban tucked under my arm. How was I to know that what I really looked like was a jerk of a hotel bearer who looked like a foreigner? And could only look suspicious, given that I was wearing horn rimmed glasses."

Not much later Bob found that being clearly identified as a foreigner had its rewards in extraordinary hospitality and friendliness. On one occasion, a store vendor near the Red Fort invited him to his rooftop home for snacks and tea and gave him an Afghan hat, which Bob wore for years. On another day, thanks to a chance meeting with students from the University of New Delhi, he ended up having not only a tour of the university, but also a picnic experience with the students at the Qtab Minar. "Man, if this was Asia," he thought, "did I love it right away, or what?"

Our enthusiasm sometimes continued to mislead us in Nepal, also, especially those of us who imagined ourselves as "going native," or trying to. Sometimes we succumbed to the self-deception that we could just fit in so well with local people that they wouldn't even notice that we were different. To minimize our obvious differences some of us wore Nepali dress from time to time, as I did at first. Such naïve and misperceived ambitions were dispelled the longer we were in Nepal. Beverly Fogg remembers getting so used to bicycling through Kathmandu, and fitting into the community by buying her food in the market, that "I forgot honestly what I must look like. I was a pale, blue-eyed blond, and I had biked down to the bazaar. And as I was bicycling one day, I glanced up at one of those wide-angle mirrors outside a store, and I saw this blond girl on a bicycle. I stopped and looked behind me to see who it was. And it was me. And I remember being dumbfounded, thinking, you fool, you thought you blended in, and look, you stick out like a sore thumb. I remember that very clearly."

Eventually the weather cleared and the DC-3 flights from Delhi to Kathmandu resumed. I was on the first flight. After we were airborne, the weather was touch and go, and only 45 minutes before our scheduled landing did the pilot announce that we would proceed to Kathmandu instead of turning around and going back to Delhi. Since none of our cables had reached Kathmandu there was no one at the airport to greet us, although Bob Bates had come out to the airport for the five previous days on the chance that we might make it. Fortunately one of our language instructors just happened to be there and took us under his wing.

Acclimatizing in Kathmandu

A week passed before the rest of the group dribbled into Kathmandu and gathered in what was virtually the only hotel in town, the Royal, simply because it was the only building in town that could accommodate nearly 80 people. The Royal was run by the renowned and eccentric former Russian ballet dancer (with Diaghilev in Paris), Boris Lisanevich. In the 1950s Boris (who at that time was operating a nightclub in Calcutta) had been invited by King

Tribhuvan to open a hotel in what the King thought was the unlikely event that tourists would come to Nepal. The King is reported to have said that Nepal was a poor prospect for tourism because there was nothing to see there.

The Royal Hotel was a huge Rana palace built in the Greco-Roman style the Ranas thought was more modern-looking than the traditional, but highly refined and sophisticated Newar architecture of the Kathmandu valley. We took our meals in the large, high-ceiling, chandeliered, baroque dining room, and occasionally had a drink at the Yak and Yeti Bar (a name which was later appropriated, after the demise of the Royal, for one of several five-star hotels which now exist in Kathmandu). At the time the only other restaurant in Kathmandu was a small, hole-in-the-wall place called the Peace Restaurant, near Peace Corps headquarters, both of them in the part of town called Lazimpat (the use of the name Peace was entirely coincidental). The Peace Restaurant was run by a kind and elderly Chinese gentleman named Wong. In later years, as Peace Corps headquarters bounced around different parts of Kathmandu, the original office, in Lazimpat, became the headquarters for Toyota in Nepal.

Meals at the Royal were accompanied by a six-man orchestra of Russian and Indian musicians (mostly string instruments with occasional brass and percussion) playing selections from their repertoire, which, we came to realize after a few days, was rather severely limited, in number if not in style—they played everything from cha-cha to Viennese schmaltz. Their favorite pieces included Strauss waltzes and, at the end of every set, a medley of American folk tunes which concluded with a stirring rendition of Old Man River.

For two weeks we continued to study the Nepali language, and attended a series of orientation classes about the history, culture, and government of Nepal. When I went to the offices of USAID for gamma globulin shots (for protection against hepatitis) I spoke to some Nepali jeep drivers, who told me I spoke better Nepali than Americans who had been working in Nepal for five years. Since my

Nepali was extremely weak at that point, their judgment could only be a comment on the lack of language skills of essentially all USAID and Embassy workers.

Ambassador Stebbins told us that the Peace Corps, along with the Embassy, USAID, and USIS, was part of the "country team," an association that was at odds with our own self-identity as a new, daring, and, above all, separate entity. He was reported to have been initially chary about having the Peace Corps in Nepal, but he proved to be a strong and sympathetic supporter by the time we arrived. At that time the American Embassy operated out of a small store-front building on the edge of the Kathmandu bazaar, near the downtown pond, Rani Pokhari. As the Ambassador was very open and friendly towards me, I would think nothing of walking into the Embassy (with no Marine guard to examine my bona fides) and walking upstairs to his office to see if he was free. The American Embassy is now, like American Embassies everywhere, a closely guarded and heavily defended fortress out on the edge of town.

Finally, the day we had long looked forward to for so long with a mixture of anticipation and dread, fear and trembling, arrived: Volunteers began leaving for their assignments. Some were assigned to various locations in Kathmandu or in nearby towns such as Patan, Bhaktapur, Banepa, and Dhulikhel. I remember driving in a truck filled with beds, stand-alone closets, and chairs to Bhaktapur (there being no furniture available in Bhaktapur, it was made and bought in Kathmandu, eight miles to the east). It seemed that half the population of Bhaktapur showed up to observe the unloading, simply because no other foreigners had lived in the town before. Other Volunteers flew off in airplanes to Pokhara, which, since it had no road connection at that time, would have been about a one week trek from Kathmandu, or to airports from which they could drive to locations in the Tarai, such as Birganj, Biratnagar, Rapti Valley, and Dharan. Some trekked to assignments in Tansen, Dhankuta, and Bhojpur. Roads have now been built to all the locations to which some of us had to trek or fly in 1962.

In spite of whatever limitations characterized our
training, we were able to arrive and hit the ground running
with no mishaps worth reporting. However, after barely a
month in Nepal Pete Johnson fell off a trail while on his first
trip from Dharan to Dhankuta in east Nepal. Making his
way along the winding, steep trail above the Tamur River,
Pete lost his footing, plunged over the edge of the trail,
and fell to the riverbed below. He was seriously injured
and unconscious, but was rescued by the Volunteers who
were accompanying him and other Volunteers who hurried
down from Dhankuta, with help from local villagers, who
refused remuneration for their assistance. Fortunately, a
helicopter eventually arrived to take him to Kathmandu.
He recovered consciousness only several weeks later in the
New York hospital to which he had been evacuated. He
was under the care of a doctor for a year, after which he
accepted another Peace Corps assignment to Malawi. He
later reported that this time, despite the fact that Malawi is
among the most mountainous countries in Africa, he lasted
the whole two years.

Education and Agriculture

In 1962, the economy of Nepal was heavily dependent
on agriculture. More than 90 percent of the population
depended on agriculture for its livelihood, 65 percent of the
GDP was contributed by the agricultural sector, and nearly
65 percent of Nepal's exports consisted of grain. There was
very little manufacturing, industry, or tourism.

Educationally the country was just beginning to develop
a school system. The Ranas had largely outlawed education,
except for a few schools for the benefit of their supporters.
Some teacher training was available, and a small college
had been built during the Rana regime, but establishing a
university was still in the discussion stage when we arrived.
It is said that when Prime Minister Chandra Shamsher
Rana approved the founding of Tri-Chandra College in
Kathmandu in 1918 he wept, because he knew it was just a

Fig. 2. Nick Cibrario conducting a class at his elementary school in Bhimphedi.

Fig. 3. Barbara Wylie teaching some of her low-caste students at the Happy Free School in Kathmandu.

matter of time before education would destroy the basis of his family's power, which was ignorance. In 1962 the overall literacy rate of the country was only 9%. Male literacy was higher, at 16%, while female literacy was barely 2%.

Faced with statistics like these, it is not surprising that the government of Nepal would have wanted Peace Corps Volunteers who could work in these two areas. Other groups in later years would also work in small business development, environment, youth development, and health, including HIV / AIDS education and awareness. But to begin with, the government of Nepal requested Volunteers who would be assigned to the two broad categories of Education and Agriculture.

These two groupings were only bureaucratically distinct, however, since some of those assigned to education were teaching agriculture, and some agriculturalists working at experimental farms and in agricultural extension functioned more as teachers. More importantly, jobs were so poorly conceived and defined that in most cases job descriptions were simply fictions or wish lists. Shop teachers were assigned to schools with not even a hint of shop facilities; agricultural specialists in dairy farming were sent to horticultural farms.

In the face of poor or non-existent job descriptions, Volunteers ended up having to find useful things to do that often had no connection with either education or agriculture. Barbara Wylie was assigned as a teacher in a girls' school but ended up starting an unofficial, after-hours school that utilized unconventional teaching methods such as those associated with Montessori. Her pupils were poor and lower caste children in her Kathmandu neighborhood who couldn't attend school during regular hours because they had to work. She started simply, by finding some chalk and some wooden boards to write on. The first day five children showed up; the next day five more came, and after a couple of months 50 students were showing up every morning, older ones helping the younger ones. Some students showed goiters beginning to grow on their throats, so Barbara asked the Peace Corps doctor to find some iodized water, which arrested them. Since the students were happy to be there, and the school was free, they named their school the "Happy Free School". This is the kind of unofficial work Volunteers did that got the attention of local children and their parents.

I was first assigned to teach English in Bhaktapur, then served for a while at the College of Education in Kathmandu, and finally went to Pharping Boarding School, just south of Kathmandu. Those were regular assignments, but I worked on a latrine-building project (in Dhulikhel, an entirely different location from my job sites) during the winter vacation period. We were building the latrine for the local high school, but we had little success in finding local people whose interest matched our own. By local standards nothing is as polluting as human excrement, and they wanted to have nothing to do with it. Such cases were typical of the impromptu way most Volunteer jobs evolved.

Those assigned to secondary schools taught English, science, mathematics, home science, geography, shop, and agriculture. Forty-one of the fifty-three education assignments were at the high school level, while twelve were college teaching positions. Some Volunteers did both, since the same building would serve different constituencies at different times of the day. For example, the hours of Bhaktapur College began at 6:30 and were over by 10:00 a.m., when I got a short break until 10:30 a.m., when the high school began its day, which ended at 4:00 p.m. As time went on some Volunteers (including me) took on responsibilities in elementary schools too, depending on local needs.

Few of the education Volunteers had taken education courses in college; in my case and that of several others, there were no education courses offered in the colleges we attended. We had even less working experience as teachers, and, as already noted, our stateside training had, astonishingly in retrospect, included no teacher training, so teaching in Nepal became an acquired skill. Doug Bingham recalls standing before something like 75 high school students his very first day at the Pokhara high school, without any teaching experience, and expected to teach in a language he had only studied for three months. It was a terrifying beginning to what turned out, over the course of two years,

Fig. 4. Jim Fisher teaching at the elementary school attached to the College of Education in Kathmandu.

Fig. 5. Joyce Thorkelson at the elementary school attached to the College of Education in Kathmandu.

Fig. 6. Gary Schaller at the village school in Banepa.

Fig. 7. Jim Fisher conducting a class outdoors at Pharping Boarding School.

to be a gratifying experience. The experience of most other Volunteers was similar to Doug's in that they ended better than they inauspiciously began.

Those of us in education were assigned to teach in Nepalese schools, at least to begin with, but the 17 Volunteers assigned to agricultural programs worked on experimental farms, in agricultural extension programs, and in agricultural research stations. One Volunteer was a skilled mechanic who worked on keeping farm equipment such as jeeps and harvesters running on a government farm. In these institutions they demonstrated mouldboard plows pulled by oxen, the use of new seed varieties, planning methods, etc., normally with Nepali government agricultural officials.

The overwhelming majority of Nepali citizens were (and still are) farmers of one sort or other, but agricultural Volunteers worked primarily with counterparts in the Nepal government, who were not farmers at all but generally urban dwellers who had been recruited and trained for careers in agricultural studies, because Nepal's economy was so heavily agricultural. One step the government had taken to diminish the gap between vocational and more academic fields was to start what were called Multipurpose High Schools. These were designed to add to the traditional academic curriculum practical vocational skills such as agriculture and shop, which were not high-status skills in Nepal.

Mike Frame had taught agriculture at Bhaktapur High School and the Dhankuta High School, but he decided at the end of his two-year agriculture assignment that the only way to understand Nepali agriculture was to work an actual farm with the resources, equipment, and implements that would typically be available to a Nepali farmer. He reenlisted for another two years to do just that, on a plot of land in the eastern hills.

The American establishment in Nepal at that time included employees in the Embassy, USAID, and USIS (United States Information Service). Virtually all of these employees lived in compounds in Kathmandu sequestered from the Nepalese community. Since a program of foreigners

Fig. 8. Les Gile showing a farm girl the chicks he has brought for her family. He bought 2,000 chicks from a local hatchery and distributed them to farmers in the Pokhara area, keeping 30 for himself. Because good feed is expensive, the typical Nepalese farmer lets his chickens peck in the dirt for themselves. Farmers became very interested in the development of Gile's chicks, which had grown much larger, after six weeks on the better diet, than their own.

working in rural Nepal was so totally new (a handful of medical missionaries had preceded us in a couple of villages, and a small band of Jesuits operated a boarding school in Kathmandu's neighboring town of Patan), officials had almost no notion of what they might request from Volunteers before their arrival, or what to expect from them after they were there. Even when Volunteers did have clear objectives, Nepalese "counterparts," who were supposed to function as local partners for Volunteers in the towns and villages where they were assigned (sometimes there were no official counterparts, or only ad hoc ones), had little idea how best to utilize their presence.

Co-teach with them? Give them their own classes to teach? I was told in Bhaktapur College and High School that I could teach whatever I wanted, as long as it was part of the national syllabus. I ended up teaching nine classes per week in the college (founded three years before I arrived) and another nine classes in the high school (about 10 years old). In some cases Volunteers showed up in towns or villages in which so-called counterparts did not even know they were coming. They had to scramble not only to create a job, but also to find living accommodations.

Because job assignments were poorly planned, Volunteers frequently switched from one job to another, on the spot, according to what local situations demanded. Peter Farquhar arrived in Pokhara and met Mr. John, an Indian immigrant who was the principal of the local college, who was expecting a chemistry teacher. Peter said, "Well, I have some chemistry background, but really, I'm a geographer." Mr. John replied, "Well, then, we'll start a geography department."

Similarly, even in the rare cases where jobs were well defined, Volunteers had to find work to do during school vacations and government holidays, which were frequent and sometimes long, particularly during the Dasain and Tihar festivals in the fall. These were the biggest Hindu festivals of the year (we were almost all assigned to predominantly Hindu communities), when schools and extension farms (such farms functioned as out-of-school education for rural people) were closed for weeks at a time. In lieu of honest fulltime jobs, which were a rarity, Volunteers were expected "to make their own jobs." For the most part, since volunteering for the Peace Corps was indicative of a somewhat proactive nature anyway, this suited the majority of Volunteers fine.

The positive result of all this is that the creativity of the Volunteers resulted in a variety of interesting work being accomplished which had not been contemplated by either Nepalese officials or Peace Corps staff. Mel Kinder had been assigned to teach agriculture in a Tarai school that had no such program, so he eventually transferred to what he considered an ideal assignment: helping keep the electrical equipment in a major health facility, Bir Hospital in Kathmandu, in working order—neither education nor agriculture. He had the skills to do this sort of work, and the hospital badly needed someone to do it. Beverly Fogg was supposed to teach home economics, but ended up working in an orphanage, which she enjoyed and where she was much appreciated. Rolf Goetze started out teaching at Public Science College, but, since he was trained as an architect, soon spent most of his time designing buildings, and even building one of them, on the campus of the college in Pokhara.

The downside is that so much back and forth in job assignments, and movements from one post to another, resulted in enormous slippage in establishing lasting social and professional relationships and a sense of lack of concrete accomplishment. I ended up in three different schools in as many locations over the course of two years, and didn't develop as enduring relationships as I might have if I had hunkered down in one place. For those who simply enjoyed being in Nepal, regardless of job satisfaction, this was not a problem. Indeed, to take an extreme example, one Volunteer so skillfully manipulated transfers from one post to another, vacation time, sick leave, and official holidays, that he spent the entire two-year tour of duty without ever staying at any job long enough to perform any useful work. He just liked being in Nepal, and he successfully gamed the system so that he could continue living there, job or no job.

Teaching and Learning

It is hard to find returned Volunteers from Nepal I who do not feel that while we were supposed to be teachers, what we were really doing most of the time was learning. Most of us felt that what we were doing—teaching, one way or the other, whether formally in classrooms or on government farms, or informally by setting an example in our domestic situations—was not totally devoid of positive benefit for the Nepalis we had set out to help. But at the same time it didn't match what we were getting out of the whole experience—learning all sorts of multiple lessons about Nepal, about the world, and most especially, almost without stop, about ourselves.

Fig. 9. Glenda Warren teaching sewing in a training school on the edge of Kathmandu.

Fig. 10. Bert Puchtler teaching carpentry at the multi-purpose high school in Pokhara.

Fig. 11. Lula Miller and two of her biology students examining a jar of pond algae that she had collected on the grounds of Tri-Chandra College in Kathmandu.

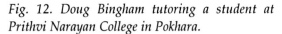

Fig. 12. Doug Bingham tutoring a student at Prithvi Narayan College in Pokhara.

Since our privileged self-identities included bringing new knowledge to undereducated people (like all Americans, we had always been told that we were "the greatest country in the world") it took us a while to realize that we were learners at least as much as we were teachers and that we didn't know everything—far from it. The whole idea of "progress" was built into the first purpose of the Peace Corps Act. We uncritically accepted that idea most of the time, but we were not entirely sure what it meant. Increase agricultural productivity? Abolish the caste system? Introduce meritocracy?

Jim Scott said the toughest thing for him was learning that he should listen to the villagers about what to do and what not to do in raising chickens and growing vegetables. He said, "If I had listened and not been so 'know-it-all' I would have saved myself a lot of time and frustration. Being in Nepal made me more mature and understanding of people. I sure needed a lot of that, too. Boy, was I a naïve and innocent dude! The farmers and market people in the bazaar were great people and taught us a great deal.

"Again, if I would listen and watch I would learn a lot in that day at the market. Those Hampshire hogs we brought in just would not mate with each other, because they were litter mates, but they mated with the native hogs. The people, the caste system, the Tibetans, farmers, shopkeepers, and villagers, the celebrations at school and on short treks away from the school, were all just fantastic. It was great to be a part of it and I find that it remains a part of me today in so many ways. I was proud to be a part of Peace Corps Nepal I."

This story tells us that not only the education Volunteers, but even the agricultural Volunteers were complete neophytes when it came to agriculture in Nepal. Everybody was at sea in this totally new environment. Jim Scott, a trained California farmer, was only marginally better off than those of us who knew next to nothing, and had his own humbling misadventures.

Since pigs were considered unclean, and anyone who raised them or ate their meat was deemed to be "untouch-

able," raising pigs put Jim in an awkward position with
the local high-caste Brahmin and Chhetri hosts and fellow
teachers in Dhankuta. Carrying them in baskets up the
mountain trail to Dhankuta made the Volunteers not only
untouchable but the laughing stock of the village. Nevertheless they persevered, convinced that pigs were suitable for
production and that this was another small way they could
make agriculture more productive (one of the Peace Corps
goals in Nepal) as well as create a chink in the armor of the
caste system (not a stated Peace Corps goal but one which
Volunteers generally regarded as progressive). Jim built several solid brick pig pens, "just like in the 'Three Little Pigs,'"
as he put it.

The pigs were also accompanied by the latest breeds of
chickens, for which the Volunteers built remarkable bamboo chicken coops in the best Peace Corps tradition. They
all failed. The pigs repeatedly escaped from their pens by
digging their way under the brick walls, and local foxes
managed to get into the chicken coops and eat the beautiful new hens and roosters. They also suffered high mortal-
ity rates from contracting local diseases. Meanwhile, the
Nepalis, laughing at all this folly, kept their chickens in
solid wood hen houses at night, and during the day let
both chickens and their own pigs roam free in the village,
where they fed themselves from scraps of grain, garbage,
or weeds and bred naturally, without the breeding con-
trols Jim attempted to instill through those elegant pig
pens and coops.

Nepali agricultural practice prevailed: The pigs and
chickens eventually ran free. Corralling efforts were abandoned, and pigs and chickens were rounded up only at
night or for requisite vaccinations. Further hilarity arose
throughout the village as the local people watched Volunteers chasing a rogue pig through every back alley and
courtyard, with even more laughter when the pig was finally wrestled down and captured right on top of Mac Odell's
own bed in the Volunteer house just off the bazaar. Experiences like these taught us a lot, and in the end Volunteers
discovered that by letting the pigs and chickens run free

we were effortlessly upgrading the local breeds, increasing production while producing new stock that were resistant to local diseases.

Sometimes teaching and learning were part of the same process. Rich Emde noticed that "*dhobis* [washerman caste] in Bhimphedi dried their laundry by spreading it out on the grass. In western culture this would make the clothing dirty, filled with germs, and germs means sickness, and animals can walk on clothing on the ground, and so forth. So I was thinking, well, there's something to be said about this. You don't have to invest in a big capital improvement; you just need a clothesline to hang so the clothes get more sunlight. But the grass would also keep air circulating from both sides, so I pulled out a notebook and made a list of the advantages and disadvantages for hanging a clothesline versus putting clothing on the grass to dry.

"Then we did some laundry ourselves and hung up a clothesline. The dhobi looked at us, like, 'These crazy Americans are doing something different.' For a couple of weeks the dhobi never used a clothesline, but a month later, sure enough he had put up a clothesline, but he still had some stuff on the ground also, so maybe he too was thinking of some advantages and disadvantages. Here we were doing the first assignment of the Peace Corps, to find a different way of doing something. He used our idea, but he didn't accept it totally. He kind of melded the two technologies together. Similarly, sometimes I've dried stuff on bushes and weeds when there wasn't a clothesline available, so here is the second Peace Corps purpose being fulfilled—learning about other ways of doing things in other places.

"Looking at different designs of how things were done, I think the experience in Nepal made my mind more open, to accept other theories of how problems can be solved, not just, you know, the western way, so to speak." As time went on, we, or at least some of us, began to recognize the tension between progress (our way) and tradition (their way)—the idea that the different ways of doing things we encountered, having withstood the test of time, might be just as good as our ways, or even better.

Ralph Teague faced different problems as a science teacher. He wanted to focus on carrying out experiments in class, which was a relatively new pedagogical approach. Sciences were taught in the school based directly on the book-based curriculum, which was set nationally by the Education Ministry and included no classroom experiments. If a topic was not specified in the official curriculum it was simply not taught. When Ralph wanted to give some instruction about a topic he thought students should know about, and give an exam on it, he hit a snag. He had to go through a rather lengthy procedure to ask for approval from the local board of education to administer an exam, even though it was a rather short and simple one. But since it was not part of the nationally approved curriculum, there was no way to include it in a regular class.

He was finally allowed to give his exam, but not before it was proofread and approved by the board of education, and it didn't count towards graduation. Performing experiments in class and giving science exams in class were basically considered to be extra-curricular events. Ralph said, "This was an element of surprise from my perspective out there. I focused on experiments performed in the classroom, with the permission of the administrators, and wanted to examine the students on that, rather than have them simply memorize by rote everything from their textbooks."

Thus the very decentralized American system was at odds with the highly centralized national system of Nepal. An accommodation was reached, but in principle neither side really gave ground, at least not then. Perhaps over time incidents like this contributed to the loosening of the hold the national system held over local schools.

George Peck had a similar, although less successful experience attempting to show students how science can explain what they experience in everyday life. Once he met a student, Ram Bahadur, in the evening for a session to explain the phases of the moon. He took two rubber balls, darkened the windows, lit his kerosene lamp to represent the sun, and showed him how the phases of the moon progressed. To see how effective this session had been, he later asked

Ram Bahadur about the phases of the moon, expecting
some reference to his explanation. Ram Bahadur considered
science in school to be an important but different world from
what he had learned growing up, and answered that the
easiest and most reliable way to find out about the phases of
the moon would be to go ask an astrologer. Thus he lived in
two worlds: He used information learned in school to pass
all-important exams; he used information available from
traditional sources to answer whatever everyday questions
might crop up. Again, an accommodation was reached for
the moment.

Of course most of our days were spent outside
classrooms. It took Volunteers a while to absorb and
understand the new worlds they were learning about
outside of the school system. For example, we were
surprised to see Nepalese men our age holding hands as
they walked down the street, and when they wanted to
show their friendship by holding hands with us, we didn't
know what to do. Holding hands in Nepal had nothing to
do with homosexuality, but still we felt uncomfortable. One
way to avoid hand holding was by carrying something so
that the hand was not available; others may have simply
gotten used to it, since we were not embarrassed as long as
other Americans didn't see us doing it.

Sometimes we did not realize what we had learned, or
done, till long after we had left Nepal. Dave Towle enjoyed
smoking some Nepali cigarettes in the Bhojpur area in east
Nepal. After he came back to the U.S. he went to a party once
and smelled something familiar, and he thought someone
in the room must be smoking Nepali cigarettes. It turns
out they were smoking *ganja* (marijuana), which Dave had
smoked in Nepal without realizing what *ganja* was.

Larry Wolfe learned lessons that altered his own
ambitions: "The people in Nepal were so gracious that you
would just respect and admire them. They're all so accepting,
free, kind, and genuine. I did not know what to expect, but
when we got there, everyone accepted us. So, it gave me a
different experience to learn about a different culture that I
had never experienced. And it gave me motivation to pursue

my education farther than I would have normally done. I think if I had not gone to Nepal, probably I would have done a bachelor's and master's of education and stopped there. I do not think I would have made the sacrifices to go on and do a doctorate if I hadn't gone to Nepal. I saw the people there that wanted to be educated so desperately, and they inspired me."

From discussions with his headmaster about the question of how much progress there had been in Nepal, Jerry Young learned a different answer from the one he had been taught in training in the U.S. "As a Peace Corps Volunteer you could see all the things that needed to be done, that needed to change, how things could change, how things could be made better. But it was painfully slow to bring about these changes. I remember having a conversation with the headmaster of my school, and we got into a discussion about progress in Nepal. I viewed progress in Nepal in terms of how far Nepal had to go; he viewed progress in Nepal in terms of how far Nepal had already come. I thought that was a real revelation, a real difference in perspective." Such frank discussions on the different assumptions each side was making gradually broke down differences in how we each saw the world.

In a similar vein, Lee Tuveson recalled, "When we were in Bhaktapur there was a young student there, Narayan Man, who used to come over to our house and engage in conversations with us. He had studied at Lumumba University in Moscow and also visited China.* This was during the height of the Cold War, so it was a unique experience to be able to talk with him. I don't think we changed anybody's minds, but at least our being there and dealing with him gave him the opportunity to meet Americans face to face. That's exactly the sort of thing that I think is worthwhile for the U.S. to engage in—individual to individual contact, and hopefully that contact with Narayan Man at least gave him a sense of the U.S., not in any

---

*   Narayan Man eventually became one of the leading Communist politicians in
      Nepal. He was not a Maoist, however, and headed his own political party, the
      Workers and Peasants Party.

propagandistic sort of way, but in a real person-to-person way. That's the only thing that I could possibly say was a contribution we made—to give him another perspective."* Such a contribution would have been welcomed politically by the American Embassy in Kathmandu, (although they would not have been aware of it), because at that time American policy was trying very hard to keep Nepal from slipping under the influence of what was then called Communist China.

What many Volunteer teachers concentrated on was not so much the specifics of this or that discipline they happened to be teaching, but the process of learning itself. Peter Grote said to his Economics students at Patan College, "'I'm going to make a mistake on purpose (this was partly to cover unintentional mistakes!), and it's going to be your responsibility to catch me on it.' So, that became a game, and there became an interaction and some independent thought. In other words, questioning of authority when authority needed to be questioned. That was something that we got into making a habit of." It was certainly not a traditional value embedded in Nepalese education.

By refusing to take self-serving explanations of cultural differences at face value, Carl Jorgensen learned a great deal: "One of the things people used to say at that time was that in Nepal the sanitation system was backwards. All of a sudden I realized, hey, their sanitation system and their concept of sanitation is like America's in the 1800s. Public health didn't come until the 1800s. There was this great tendency to romanticize the European past, relative to the past of third world peoples and to take what was a difference of a few decades and turning it into centuries. I learned that." Carl here expresses a view of history and culture that we all assumed much of the time—the idea that cultural difference is linear and can be placed on a

---

* This other perspective was part of the second purpose of the Peace Corps—to give an accurate impression of what America was and had to offer. Narayan Man thus got a different impression from that given in a letter to the editor of the pro-Soviet Nepali weekly, *Samikshya*, in 1964: "The main aim of the Peace Corps program is to incite the Nepalese people against the Soviet Union and China, countries that are friends of ours."

Fig. 13. Becky Murphy teaching a class in home science at Pokhara High School.

Fig. 14. Bob Proctor teaching a botany class at Tri-Chandra College, in Kathmandu.

steadily improving progressive sequence of events and organization.

Carl continued, "One point that's very interesting is how hard it is to understand what a culture is really about. I mean, you remember people were telling us, 'Well, the men rule this culture.' But then we found out that the women controlled the money for the *pujas*. Well, if you control the household income, that's a hell of a lot of control in the family. But we never got close enough to the Nepalis to understand them.

"Something else that was very intriguing was when Lee, our roommate, grew very thin. You remember what the Nepalis told him he had to do? They said, 'You've gotten very thin. We're really worried about you. We need to find a woman for you. You need to go visit a prostitute.' The idea was that he was getting sick because he was an adult man, and he wasn't having sex. This made him sick, and he was getting thin. It was a real medical problem, and they said he had to go see a prostitute.

"I mean, we had been told, you know, that everything was within marriage in Nepal, and obviously it wasn't. So you get these hints of what was different, but we never found out all about it. I found out enough about it to allow me, again, both in my life and in my teaching, to talk to students about how one has to be really cautious about presuming that one understands a culture or accepting these ideas such as, well, that everything's for the men."

Volunteers sometimes had mixed feelings about the cultural differences they encountered. Their eyes might be opened to a new and valuable way of life, but that way of life was not above critique either. Dick Murphy said, "When I was a college graduate, I had studied and read and understood the foibles and things that were less than optimum in my own society back home. When I got to Nepal, I really began to understand, and it was rather enlightening, to see things, to understand the things that were right in the way that the United States is run and the way the people in the U.S. support and play a role in the government and the society.

"The impact of being in Nepal made such a big difference that I decided I'd like to try to share this revelation, and figured one of the ways I might do that would be to teach, maybe at the secondary level. Before that, I had never considered teaching—in fact, if someone had told my high school classmates that I was going to be a teacher, that would have been the biggest laugh going."

He added, "I was able to bring in aspects of what I'd picked up in Nepal. For instance, the pipal tree planted in a stone rectangle. I described to my students how much effort was necessary to build that rectangle, to fill it up with soil— all by hand, including stones that had to be carried down from the hills, soil had to be scooped up and tossed into this big, cavernous opening. Then a tree planted.

"People then would come by, relax, place their load on the wall underneath the tree and take a break from the hot sun and think good thoughts about the person who had put all the effort into making this shady, restful spot. Whoever had built the resting place would accumulate some merit that way. I told my students, you don't always have to have accolades for what you do. You might want to do something just because you can rack up a little bit of merit. You don't have to have the personal recognition for it.

"The most enjoyable aspect of living in Nepal was the personal relationship with my co-worker, and interaction with the people. It was hard for me to understand, at first, how people who had so little could be so happy. That was a revelation. It provided a kind of background, which Becky and I used throughout our lives, to distinguish between what you need and what you want—a big factor of that came out of the Peace Corps for me, personally. I didn't have to buy into all the consumerism in the States." So Dick was simultaneously critical and admiring of different aspects of life in Nepal, and that could be said of any of us.

In another attempt to learn about a different way of life, Dan Pierce once "went native" on a visit to fellow PCVs in Tansen, and from there walked on to Pokhara. "I tried to do this 'native' style and bought a basket with a tump line across my forehead to hold the basket on my back. My load wasn't much more than a sleeping bag, spare clothes, and some food. I stayed at tea houses at night, sleeping on a little straw. I didn't try to do it barefoot. I found that carrying a basket on your back with minimal straps and a line around your forehead must be something you have to grow up with because it was decidedly uncomfortable for me. It was worth it just for the amused looks I got from the Nepalis who saw this tall paleface carrying a basket on his back."

Not all teaching took place in a classroom. When Mark and Suki went trekking, in response to questions about where America was, they would draw maps in the dirt; a big circle for Nepal, wiggly lines for "the big water" and another big circle for America.

Glenda Warren always tells people that to her, living in Nepal as she did "must be what it feels like to be a baby when they are getting accustomed to the people, the food, the clothing, the holidays, the weather—everything was new. But the only difference is, we were old enough to recognize that we were learning something. That's why I think that we could learn more than we could teach."

All these examples demonstrate a very open and largely nonjudgmental way of thinking about the experiences we were undergoing, unlike the smug, know-it-all, autocratic attitudes of American teachers in the Philippines half a century before;[40] a willingness to listen to local people and their attitudes was a radical departure from its very beginnings. There was certainly an element of "showing the natives how to live better," but that attitude was always tempered by the realization that events of daily life were showing Volunteers that they were far from having all the answers.

Dave Sears summed it up this way: "We were pretty naïve. We expected things to happen pretty fast. We were going to save the world. We were ready to go, to change the world. The world turned out to be difficult to change. In the end, we were the ones who were changed."

Rewards and Travails

At the final evaluation conference in Nepal, which took place at the end of the two years of service, in May, 1964, Volunteers were asked if, after they returned home, they expected problems in their job or schooling, family, friends, or life style. Volunteers answered overwhelmingly that

Fig. 15. Jim Fisher, playing barker, raffles off a chicken to raise money for a boy's school in Kathmandu.

they expected no problems in any of these areas. Thus, Volunteers left Nepal with considerable self-confidence in their ability to get on with social and professional life and its challenges. In terms of total satisfaction, asked if, knowing what they then knew, they would volunteer again to serve in the Peace Corps, 52 (i.e., all who attended the conference) said yes, none said no.

Later, Bob Proctor wrote, "It's very difficult to particularize the rewards of the experience in Nepal. There are many, and they tend to overlap. Let me begin with fellow Volunteers. To say that it was initially a little hard to relate to many of them, never mind 'like' them, would be diplomatic. I just couldn't imagine in those early weeks of training getting along with such individuals. Well, time and circumstances, harsh ones often, sure changed that. Let's say that in that two-year period perhaps some of the most enduring friendships of my life were forged with some of the most unlikely people...It's been a great group of people, and it has been my privilege to be one of them. I suppose we all contributed to each other's world awareness. We all benefited through interaction with each other, and it's continued over the years. That has been one of the pleasures of my life.

"Related to this, of course, were the friendships formed with Nepalis, especially with a number of students, that still flourish decades later. I also still have some very good Nepali friends that I first met back in '62 and '63. They have enriched my life and continue to do so."

A reward of a different kind was that of "place." Bob went on to describe "an appreciation of a people and a country and a part of the world that, however exotic, nevertheless became part of me, part of my consciousness, part of my concerns about the nature of life and destiny. I found I could actually love 'my' counterparts and students, and in spite of vast cultural differences, be one with them in many ways. It was an exhilarating—and humbling—experience. And a most unexpected reward."

In a similar vein, Bob Murphy said, "Growing up in Wisconsin, I had not traveled. I was relatively provincial, but the Peace Corps opened the doors, it opened my eyes. It made me realize that there are other cultures out there, that I could interchange with other cultures, which I did in subsequent positions. But the Peace Corps experience was crucial."

Jane Stevens says that evaluating the rewards depends on whether you're looking at the experience now or then. "Back then, I think I was always sort of overwhelmed at how the Nepalis took us at face value and always incorporated us into their culture and lifestyles and looked out for our best interests and certainly made us feel like we were really the guests of honor. We were always treated in that manner. I think that we were brought in as sort of poor young Americans and always treated with great respect and appreciation.

"Now, we have to look back at what the Peace Corps was really established for—for young Americans to go out and share our knowledge and skills with folks of different cultures. But we all know that what we learned and what we brought back was much greater than anything we ever taught or did, and I think the farther we get away from that experience, the more I realize that what we learned about the cultures in which we were living and the things we were doing and the people we met, were clearly the benefits. For the most part, we were the beneficiaries of this experience."

Ralph Teague said his and Sam Hunt's situation in Birganj, a large Tarai city, was quite different from that of most other Volunteers. They were given a new, *pakka* (cement) house to live in, and they taught in a large, relatively well-equipped high school. They were invited to local organizations such as cricket clubs, a very different kind of situation neither of them was really used to. They had expected to be Peace Corps Volunteers in some of the most remote areas of the country, and here they were in one of the larger towns and among some of the respected elite in the town.

Amidst all the adulation he received from his relatively high class hosts, Ralph felt that more education classes would have made the praise more justified. He was asked what skills he used in teaching, what teaching method he used, but those who asked those questions didn't realize he had never taught a class in his life. Without any formal education degree or teaching experience, like other Volunteers he just had to face up to that at some level and carry on as if he were the expert they thought he was, even if he knew he wasn't.

This criticism was leveled not only by the Volunteers themselves at themselves, but also by critics of the United States and the Peace Corps at the time. At the height of the Cold War, it is not altogether surprising that this sentiment was expressed in a letter to the editor in 1964 of a pro-Soviet Nepali weekly, *Samikshya:*

"American aid is pouring into Nepal, not for the development of the country, but to safeguard American interests. The self-interest of American capitalists is hidden behind the Peace Corps objectives. The Volunteers are not needed in Nepal since they are not experts. We already have enough laborers in our country."

Despite the generalized gusto that was pervasive during our time in Nepal, upon later reflection we ourselves began to develop some doubts, and not all Volunteers were entirely sold on the Peace Corps idea. Mel Kinder developed the view that it would be much more efficient, if we're going to have relationships with third world countries, that we bring their citizens to the U.S.—Vietnamese, Thai, Chinese, Africans, etc. He said, "When they come here, we can develop a relationship, one society to another, based upon family and really close economic ties. The Peace Corps idea that we are going to educate Americans to live in the third world is not realistic. I mean, sure, it helps, it's education, but not in terms of having a big impact on what's going on, you know. The Peace Corps in India has not had nearly as much impact as Indians coming here and working and building those kinds of things."

Sometimes the rewards were of a non-native variety. Joyce had been in Nepal six months or so when the U.S. Marine guards arrived in the country. Until their arrival there were no Americans guarding the Embassy (which was housed in a small, store-front building near downtown Kathmandu), so the Marines were assigned that duty; whenever the Embassy was closed, they stood guard over it. Joyce said, "They used to have parties on Friday afternoons. That was great. They had all the new music, food. If two people showed up that was enough to make it a party. So we got to know those guys very well. I ended up marrying one of them."

The positive returns were often a long time coming. Lee Tuveson's views of the rewards of living and working in Nepal became apparent only after many years of thinking about it: "It's only revealed itself after years of coming out of it, but to me the most rewarding part was the introduction to a foreign culture. When I look back on my own life, coming from a Midwestern background, no one in my family had been overseas, the whole Peace Corps experience turned out to be very much a watershed event in my life. It's hard to identify any particular event, because it was the totality of the experience that turned out to be most rewarding. Among other things was the sense of self-reliance, almost an arrogance, you know, that, geez, I can do anything now because I've lived in a village in Nepal and have gone through an extraordinary experience, a cross-cultural experience, and I adapted successfully to that environment. So it was the totality of the experience that was so rewarding."

Dave Towle's appreciation of his experience embraced a wide spectrum of qualities: "I loved the mountains. I enjoyed being in Kathmandu, or in the Tarai, and I loved being up in the hills. The people I met there for the most part were very friendly and supportive. I think in terms of personal growth it was the idea that you could do things on a much different scale than I had been brought up to believe. That it was possible to live happily in a simple kind of environment. Simple in terms of housing, and facilities, but complex in terms of culture."

For Jerry Young, also, the time in Nepal opened a whole new world: "I think the best part about it was just the opportunity to experience the things I had never experienced before, the cross-cultural experiences. Living in a part of the world that wasn't Christian, that was Hindu-Buddhist, and drawing into question all the things that I had learned and knew about growing up in rural southern Michigan. Questioning what could be, the possibilities of what could be.

"I think of what the experience did for me. It was just a fantastic experience, making me a better citizen, a better person. It certainly made me more tolerant, more understanding of other cultures and philosophies. Also, it really cemented my natural instinct to be adventurous. I have probably been more adventurous through the years since then than I would have been, because I had that experience. I realized what meaning adventure could have in one's life."

For Nick Cibrario, the most rewarding part of life in Nepal was learning the language and getting to know the people of Nepal. "To me, that is the heart of it—communicating, sharing, talking about things. Sometimes they'd be very challenging about what was going on in the world. But getting to know, interact—that was the most meaningful to me. And not just with the Nepalis, but with your fellow Volunteers, who could come and stay overnight at your house. That was all part of it. Feeling very close to people, to the Peace Corps Volunteers that were working here, strong feeling toward the people—I treasure all these memories."

One of the rewards for Carl Jorgensen was learning how to relax: "At first I think, here I was introduced somewhat to Asian philosophies of religion; the aspects of Buddhist philosophy, which have influenced me in my life, and that certainly started here. Certainly I learned how to relax more here. The bus was supposed to come at three. It was going to show up somewhere between three o'clock and nine o'clock—maybe. So you have to live your life, well that bus is coming—maybe. I learned to do that, and to be very comfortable with that."

Dan Pierce reported, "Living in Nepal, and especially the time I was working with the malaria eradication program in the Rapti Valley, made me appreciate how little one needed in material goods to live, and apparently to live a reasonably satisfying life. It still gives me pause when I am surrounded by all manner of goods in a typical U.S. shopping mall.

"I think that being in Nepal sensitized me to the diversity of cultures and people. Even though I had traveled in Europe and lived in Finland and Germany, Nepal was sufficiently different from western culture to have a larger impact."

There was also a social benefit for Dan in having been in the Peace Corps. As in the other rewards people felt listed above, this one had not been anticipated: "Being in the Peace Corps in Nepal probably helped me on return in meeting people and in dating, because it made me seem a little exotic and more interesting."

Travails

Somewhat surprisingly, in view of a fair amount of chronic complaining while we were in Nepal, there was a general tendency to discount or dismiss, decades later, whatever hardships or difficulties or frustrations we had encountered while "in country." The sentiment was often expressed that while we might have griped about things then, time had dimmed those negative memories. In classic psychological tradition, we accentuated the positive memories and repressed the negative ones. Even when specifics could be listed, I had the feeling from interviews that remembering the negatives took much more head-scratching—and took much longer—than it did to produce a list of the positives.

Much of the time we were not having particularly positive or negative experiences, but merely trying to get through days filled with things we didn't understand, or understood only dimly. Mimi Smith doesn't remember any particular highs or lows, but rather being in a more or less continuous state of culture shock for the first year or so she was in Nepal. Things like plastering their house floor with a mixture of cow dung and water was something she'd never heard of or even imagined, but learned about by necessity.

Nevertheless, at the final evaluation conference just before leaving Nepal, asked about a list of 29 problems they might have experienced, only three problems were defined by double-digit numbers of Volunteers as "serious problems." Lack of support from host country officials, or lack of activity of host country nationals in helping themselves, were listed most frequently (11 and 12 times, respectively) as serious problems. Even in these cases, however, 23 and 29 Volunteers, respectively (out of 52) regarded them as only "minor problems," while 22 and 11 thought they were "no problem at all."

The only other comparable "serious problem" mentioned was dating (12 times), and ten considered dating only "a minor problem," with 29 counting dating as "no problem at all." In this context "problem" can be construed to mean lack of eligible dating partners, such as other Volunteers or Marine guards at the Embassy. The possibility of "dating" Nepalis simply didn't arise in the social and cultural context of Nepal at that time, although one Volunteer did end up marrying a Sherpa, from the hills of eastern Nepal, during her second tour. By now so many Nepali/foreigner marriages have taken place (including those involving Volunteers) that it would be impossible to count them.

By contrast, in a long list of 26 other possible problems ranging from health, food, and medical care to relationships with Nepalis or other Peace Corps Volunteers, all were considered by large numbers to be "no problem at all." The complete list of 29 possible problems is as follows:

Image of the Peace Corps held by host country nationals
Support from Peace Corps officials in host country
Support from host country officials
My ability to communicate in the local dialect
Ability to see results
Living allowances
My technical skills for the job
Keeping the problem Volunteers in the country
Number of visits from the staff
Health
Food
Under-friendliness of the local people
Housing-living arrangements
Interest of host country in Peace Corps work
Physical hardships

Effective working counterpart
Medical care
Absence of challenge in the role of PCV
Excessive social demands by host country nationals
Activity of host country nationals in helping themselves
Isolation in living or work situation
Frustrating work experiences
Dating
Giving all you could to the whole job of being a Volunteer
Peace Corps policies
Relationship with other expatriates
Relationships with other PCVs
Variation in skills of Volunteers in this group
Transportation

Interestingly, not a single Volunteer considered housing-living arrangements, friendliness of local people, physical hardships, relationships with other expatriates, or relationships with other Volunteers to be serious problems.

One area where some consensus existed concerned the ability to communicate in the Nepali language. Of 51 who answered this question, 12 felt they had a good command of the language (plus one who claimed excellent command), while 38 felt they had only a fair, marginal, or poor command of the language. The importance of this deficiency is reflected by the 48 who felt that command of the local language was of some or great importance—only three felt it to be of very little importance, and none felt it was of no importance.

Proctor put the everyday problems we encountered in perspective this way: "Sure, it was easy to nearly despair sometimes about demonic Delhi Bellies, or almost cry for the lack of a frosty cold beer. But these, and similar 'body deprivations' invariably paled in contrast to 'body delights.' Every waking hour invariably involved an almost overwhelming feast for the eye, the ear, even the nose (the fragrance of sandalwood could and did pervade the uriniferous alleys of the city). I used to spend hours, literally, standing unobtrusively in the shadows of a shop in Asan Tole, watching, listening, breathing in the voluptuousness of the swirl of humanity passing by. And food! Dal-bhat-tarkari [lentils-rice-vegetables]! Who would guess that *to this day* I enjoy this combo with a relish that defies description."

A frequently recurring theme was the discouragement felt at the slow pace of change and lack of accomplishments. Yet for Gary Schaller, there was little to complain about, compared to the rewards. The slow pace of change was frustrating, he admitted, but in retrospect he also wonders why he expected sudden change in a society that had existed and persisted for hundreds of years.

Joyce Thorkelsons's main difficulty was with: *"bholi-parsi"* [tomorrow—the day after tomorrow]. That was so frustrating. Yes, tomorrow, tomorrow. You'd be ready for action, but it wouldn't happen till tomorrow. It was, like, I want to do it now, I'm ready now. And, unfortunately, you hear it so much that when the second year rolls around you're resigned to waiting for that. You lose the urgency to do something. Maybe that is better because then you fit more into their lifestyle, and their way of doing things. I know it was awfully frustrating.

"I remember we didn't want to associate with Americans in the beginning. We just wanted to associate with Nepalis— that was part of the Peace Corps style. After a while we fell back into our old patterns. It was nice to go to the American Club, or see an American movie, once in a while. I did see my share of Hindi movies as well. I had my Nepali friends who took me there. And I still enjoy Hindi movies." Even here, thinking about and enumerating negatives, Joyce ends up on a positive note.

For Mark and Suki Schroeder, in everyday life there was nothing in particular to complain about. The sole complaint they had was the one many experienced: the bureaucratic muddle. As they put it, "There was lots of political infighting at the Agriculture Ministry, so much so that towards the end everything fell apart, and many officials left for foreign countries or other assignments."

Jane Stevens admits that at the time we all felt that we experienced some hardships and were making some sacrifices. But in retrospect, those appear to be pretty minimal. "I had a two-day walk to my village. We had no showers, no refrigeration, no electricity, no heat, and we did just fine. We all came through it in great shape and didn't lose much weight, learned some language, certainly had a chance to read a lot of great books as well as make some wonderful friends, got to see a part of the world we never would have seen otherwise, and some sort of appreciation for a totally different and eastern culture. There were the usual hardships, but they never seemed to really get in the way of life.

"I was in a pretty good situation, we enjoyed it, we never seemed to have any problems that were unsolvable, and so we had a village situation where it was very safe, very refreshing. Lots of folks came to visit. We got mail a couple of times a month. We ordered cases of ketchup from India because we had pretty much a rice diet, but we seemed to find that if we ate our rice with ketchup, it was tolerable, so we ordered cases of ketchup."

One incident perhaps sums up our reactions to difficulties we confronted in Nepal. Peace Corps headquarters in Washington used to publish a newsletter-type magazine (monthly) with articles on how the Peace Corps assignments were being experienced and handled in different countries. I remember once sitting around with a few other Volunteers reading and discussing an article in this magazine about Volunteer living conditions in the Philippines. A Volunteer had written that one of the problems was that it was hard to find cold cokes. Our immediate, uniform, and astonished reaction was: "They have cokes?" He also wrote that it was hard to keep the glass windows in their houses clean. Our amazed reaction was, again: "They have glass windows?" Or, his complaint that at certain times of day taxis were hard to find. To which we riposted: "They have roads?"

The fact is that we took pride in the hair-shirt existence into which we had plunged. We had to do without many of the amenities of life we were used to, but that seemed to make the entire experience more authentic and even more enjoyable. To a certain extent, that was the whole point. Thatched roofs, lack of electricity, no plumbing, walking for days to reach a destination because there were no roads—that's what many of us had wanted, what drew us to the Peace Corps and/or Nepal in the first place. We were eager to experience a truly different way of life, and it wasn't hard to do. Most of the time, it was unavoidable.

What was surprising is how quickly, even effortlessly, we took to Nepal, loved it, and made it "our" country and our home, warts and all. On December 13th 1962, I made the following entry in my daily journal, from my post in Bhaktapur, eight miles east of Kathmandu:

"Six months ago today I joined the Peace Corps. That means that 25% of my time is up. I have mixed reactions to being here in Nepal, 12,000 miles away from home. Objectively, the contrast between this year and last could not be greater. I am now a teacher, instead of a pupil; I live in an unheated house with no water, and I eat little but rice; last year I lived in a Gothic building in a room with a fireplace, and I was served excellent meals three times a day. This year entertainment consists of walking around town, or a bike ride to Kathmandu, or a picnic in the country. Last year entertainment consisted of football games, dances, parties, all on a lavish scale, even by American standards.

"Yet subjectively, I feel right now as if I have always lived here. Nothing seems more natural than to teach a class in a freezing room at 6:40 in the morning, or to eat rice day after day after day with little else. Subjectively, I feel no "culture shock", and I feel right at home. Officially, I am a teacher, but I think I am learning more now than I ever did in school or college. This has been an exciting and vastly rewarding experience."

If we helped people too, so much the better, but if we didn't, we still had the self-satisfaction of, first: being free from the pressures we were used to in the U.S., and second: living the way we wanted to live, to feel as free as we did, to be on the cutting edge of a new phase in international and intercultural relations, remaking the world into a better place, or so we thought. So, what at one level was deprivation, at another was satisfaction and vindication at living a life-style we had consciously and explicitly sought. We had found what we were looking for.

To revel in successfully confronting the lack of creature comforts we were used to is one thing, but that should not mask our darker times, for it is also true that we experienced moments of depression and loneliness, culminating sometimes in despair. In the final, end-of-service conference, asked if they had experienced emotional low points during their time in Nepal, 44 replied yes, and only five said no.

Sometimes something small could trigger memories of what life was like at home, and spark a hunger for it—like Proust's madeleine cookies. Mike Frame wrote that he walked to a part of his town where he hadn't been before, and then on out into the country, where there was a spring-like fresh breeze, "and the air smelled so good that it made me a little homesick. It reminded me of the times in the spring at home when the snow had melted and the ground had just dried off enough in the pasture to lie down on it, but there would still be water running in the valleys. It was just like that here; the trees were bare; the fields were brown except for fields of green wheat where there was irrigation water available."[41]

Bernie Snoyer noticed that whenever we talk about Nepal, as we do when we see each other, at reunions or elsewhere, we tend to dwell on rousing stories which accentuate the positive and are fun to remember and relate. The 44th reunion, held in Minnesota in 2006, could be described, without much exaggeration, as a three-day, non-stop Laugh-In. Like soldiers, ironically, we love our war stories. But no one wants to express how we conquered loneliness or depression, or how we felt about missing our families or someone we left behind whom we loved, and what helped us through the kinds of feelings we experienced during those occasional bleak, joyless, and downhearted days.

5

NEPALIS GLOBALIZING AND GLOBALIZED

Impact at the Time

There are several reasons why it is difficult to assess the impact of Volunteers on Nepal. Some obvious ones include the difficulty of tracing, over decades and generations, the impact of small events. Another is the gradual disappearance of most of the people Volunteers knew, as people move around and die or, more generally, simply lose touch. Over time, communication has slowly ground to a halt. This became evident at the reunion in Nepal in 2000. As just one example, when I went out to see how the school latrine we built in Dhulikhel looked, I couldn't find it. It had long since been plowed under, to make way for other buildings in an expanding hill bazaar town. Only after several hours of searching and questioning was I able to find anyone who even remembered it, and he took me to the hillside and showed me where it had been. It had disappeared without a trace. How soon they forget.

Another reason it is hard to get a handle on what effect Volunteers had on Nepal is that they grew increasingly cautious in making claims about it. "As to what difference our being in Nepal made to those people in Tansen, I think we have to be sort of humble about that," Jane Stevens said. "Hopefully, we helped them gain some better level of understanding of Americans, what we are like, what our purposes were, and that was certainly one of the things we wanted to get across. At that time Nepal was a neutral country, and politically it sort of had a place in the Cold War. I think we were trying to influence folks toward our way of thinking as opposed to maybe what the Soviets were putting out. We were making a pitch for a free world sort of approach to life, but what did we do for them? We maybe helped some young people learn English. We certainly tried to set up a household that had a "living by demonstration" effect, in terms of how to eat better, do some basic things in terms of health care and sanitation, and I think probably living-by-demonstration was maybe the best thing we did."

Bob Proctor is also cautious about measuring the effect of his time in Nepal on Nepal: "In my heart of hearts, I do not know what effect I had. I can point to various friendships that endure. If their lives have been positively affected by me, well and good. But with few exceptions those people are no longer in Nepal, and haven't been for many years. We are in the process of passing, and even this legacy will soon be gone.

"But does Nepal itself benefit? I don't think so. And yes, on return visits to Kathmandu, it was always satisfying to be remembered by former colleagues at Tri Chandra College, and later, by Nepalese USIS and Embassy staffers; by a few people in the Nepalese press who remembered our cordial relationships, and by the now very senior members of families I once knew well when teaching their children English. I must have touched these people deeply; they sure touched me.

"That said, collectively—and feedback over the years confirms—that our group had a tremendous impact however it might be measured or described. I even had one former student, now an officer of the World Bank, tell me that he and his generation always considered our group to be THE Peace Corps group. None of our successor groups could measure up to us. That's fine. But what is the long-term legacy in the larger picture of things? If it is big, it must be subtle enough, or modest enough, as to be nearly invisible. If it is small, well, it is that, and nothing more."

One of the Dhankuta teachers, Mac Odell, learned that his ignorance of Nepali agriculture did not detract from significant agricultural accomplishments, but it took him years to realize that. When he and Barbara went to reform elementary education in Solu, they made school gardens a part of everything they did. Members of a church in Greene, NY, sent them bundles of vegetable and flower seed packets, on the assumption that the climate in upstate NY was similar to that in Solu, which turned out to be not a bad guess. The seeds, in their colorful packets, were a great hit, and both students and their parents clamored for them. Similarly, when local farmers persuaded them, on the basis of their own visits to Darjeeling (which boasted a similar climate), that apples could be a successful crop in Solu, they lobbied Peace Corps, USAID, and the Ministry of Agriculture to send out apple seedlings to try out.

Ten porter-loads of seedlings were sent out from Kathmandu on the ten-day overland trek to Phaplu, their village in Solu. Although many died on the way, enough survived to be planted by enthusiastic farmers who confirmed that they would grow well. Mac and Barbatra then persuaded the Peace Corps doctor, who came out by helicopter for their 6-monthly check-ups, to bring as many apple seedlings as the helicopter could carry, and quickly found themselves with over 1,000 seedlings. They became very popular among the farmers.

Knowing the limitations of their agricultural knowledge (neither Mac nor Barbara had any agricultural background), and realizing that their school gardens would suffer badly during the winter holidays, they decided to make all extra seeds and seedlings available to local farmers—for a price. Consulting with their local friends, they set the prices high enough to indicate their real value, and to raise money for their own school projects. To their amazement, people came out of the woodwork with fistfuls of cash to get hold of the seeds and seedlings. When asked how to plant and care for them, and looking back on their Dhankuta pig and chicken fiascos, they said: "We have no idea. We can read you what it says on the packets. But otherwise you people have been farming here for generations. You know much better how to grow things than we do. Use your own best judgment."

Impact over the Long Haul

Since they were not there for a long time, they rarely saw the full fruits of these ventures, though they did see a few vegetables and flowers grow in the school gardens. They also saw some spinach, carrots, and flowers appear in a few local gardens. Of course, the apple seedlings would take years to bear fruit. They trusted the local farmers and hoped for the best, but they knew they would be unlikely to see the real outcomes of these experiments.

Years later, coming back to Nepal on a "honeymoon" trip with his new wife, Marcia, they made their way first to Phaplu. On arrival they were greeted by old friends who immediately wanted to show off their apple orchards, acres and acres of apple trees, bearing beautiful apples. Local shops were full of apples, and new restaurants featured apple pie, apple pancakes, and apple cider, some of it nicely fermented into a very pleasant wine.

The vegetables and flowers were another story. They'd seen little come of all those seed packets distributed earlier. The climate was apparently too harsh; not quite like Greene, NY, after all. Trekking north into the colder Khumbu region, where little except potatoes was growing in the 1960s, they were surprised to find bountiful vegetable gardens and flowers blooming all along the trail. Closer inspection revealed that local farmers and lodge owners were raising seedlings under plastic, using bamboo hoops to create marvelous little "hot houses." Clearly they had learned new techniques Mac had never known, and certainly not introduced with his seeds.

Curious to find the source of this know-how, and the seeds that seemed so well adapted to this harsh climate, they asked the local people where they got their seeds and new technology. "Oh, just up the trail at the Japanese Farm." Knowing that the Japanese were perhaps the cleverest vegetable growers in the world, he secretly envied the fact that they had been able to bring about an agricultural revolution in the Khumbu region that he had not.

Eager to learn the secrets of their success, however, Mac tracked down the Japanese volunteer who was operating the demonstration farm. "Where did you find the seeds adapted to this climate?" he asked, innocently. "Oh, that was the easy part," he replied. "Some American who was here years ago distributed a lot of seeds. The local people planted them, cared for them by growing them in little cups on their window sills, brought them in at night, and carefully selected and propagated those that grew, until they had seeds adapted to this climate. By themselves, the local farmers had done seed selection research that would otherwise have cost a million dollars. Then I took these seeds, showed them how to make "hot houses" from plastic and bamboo, how to make and use compost, and watched them produce a horticultural revolution here in the valley, as you can see. Now they are supplying fresh vegetables and flowers to the growing tourism industry, local restaurants and hotels. They're quite prosperous now."

The issue here is not about bringing knowledge by educated PCVs who know more than Nepalis, or Nepalis who know more than naïve PCVs, but rather what happens when people of contrasting backgrounds and experiences try to accomplish common goals. Mac and Barbara were largely ignorant about agriculture, but their ignorance had not prevented some success, which was achieved simply by introducing things (e.g., seeds) they didn't know much about but which local people, who were immensely interested in and knowledgeable about agriculture, could capitalize on. Local farmers already had the knowledge, and only needed the novelties outsiders (whether PCVS, Nepalis or visitors from other countries) could provide. This example also shows that some of the effects PCVs had on Nepal were unforeseen by Volunteers themselves—not intended exactly at the time, but bearing fruit much later, long after they had gone home. Meanwhile, others, from other parts of the world (in this case, Japan), had come to do their own bit of globalizing. The case of the new veggie seeds illustrates that the impact Volunteers had could not always be quantified or described in very concrete terms, and also that our presence produced effects that would not become apparent for many years. In the vast majority of these cases, we still don't know what we did or did not get done.

Mike Frame discovered this gradually during his later jobs in Nepal. After his four years as a Volunteer (two of them when he reenlisted at the end of his first tour to work his own farm), Mike spent two years working in the agricultural program for USAID in Nepal. He returned to Nepal in 1980 on a five-year stint in charge of agricultural programs for the Peace Corps, which gave him a different perspective from what he had developed as a Volunteer 20 years earlier. He said, "[As a staff person] I would go and talk to a lot of district officers in all these districts. I got into about 60 districts, out of the total of 75 districts in the country. Several times some of the brightest and the most forward-looking of these district officers had been in a school where a Peace Corps Volunteer had taught. Of course, we were in the main district schools in those days, when we were first there. But a lot of these officers said, 'Do you know so-and-so who was a Peace Corps Volunteer?' He had gotten a lot of support from this or that Volunteer. That's one thing I haven't heard mentioned otherwise, you know. I made this observation that a great deal of the Peace Corps impact has taken many years to incubate and develop, and it was a very long time in coming to fruition."

The reward of feeling that one had accomplished something, done something of benefit to Nepalis, was the most sought and most difficult feeling to attain. It is difficult to measure such influences without the views of those who felt the impacts of Volunteers, and these are mostly unavailable; evaluators from Washington never asked to talk to our Nepali friends and co-workers. One can infer a positive influence from the way friendships developed then and have continued over the years, but it would be a rare occasion indeed when a Volunteer teacher would have the chance to quiz a former student on his impact.

In one case I'm aware of, however, this did happen. In 1975 Flemming Heegaard was back in Nepal, eleven years after he had left it. As it happened, a Sherpa wedding was going on in Kathmandu to which he had somehow ended up being invited. He reported, "I went there. I didn't know anybody, but then I asked who the groom was. They said, 'Oh, that's the guy sitting over there with his wife on the sofa.' I went over to him. I said, 'Are you the one who's getting married today? Are you the groom?' He said, 'Yeah.' Then he looked at me again, did a double take, and then said, 'You were sent from God.' I said, 'Excuse me?' He said, 'Yeah, you were my teacher at Balaju Boarding School. I was the only Sherpa there.' I said, 'Of course, I remember you. That's great.'

"Then I said, 'By the way, what was the impact that we had at that time? I mean, you were one of those boys there.' He replied, 'Oh, it was incredible. You came in and you started to get us all involved in fixing up the school, putting in electricity, fixing up the kitchen, and so on. We had nothing. We couldn't study because we had no kerosene. We had no electricity. The way you turned the school into a community development project and got us working was fantastic. All the students thought so. I certainly think so.'"

What stories there are like this are, by their very nature, difficult to find. A Volunteer from Dhankuta, who returned decades later, visited Mac when he was working in Kathmandu. "Mac," he said, "Do you know what an effect we had on the caste system in Dhankuta?" Recalling their earlier fiascos with pigs and chickens (see pp. 91-92), and how almost no one in the village would take food from them, Mac thought it unlikely they'd made a dent. "Well," he said, "I discovered that those shop classes you taught had an impact that I just saw during my recent visit. You might remember that the high school, while largely consisting of Brahmin and Chhetri students, did have some untouchable Carpenter and Blacksmith children attending on scholarship. And you recall how you brought local Blacksmiths and Carpenters into the school to show the children how they made their tools— tools that you purchased and used for those shop classes. Well, apparently seeing their parents' skills honored before classrooms full of Brahmins and Chhetris brought great pride to the Blacksmith and Carpenter children.

Some of those untouchable students decided to use their education to help establish businesses—mechanical and cabinet-making businesses. As Dhankuta grew, the demand for these services grew and these businesses became quite successful. One leading Blacksmith not only became prosperous with his new mechanical trade but was ultimately elected to the town council. He became quite a respected citizen, his daughter got a good education, and now he has opened a computer shop in Dhankuta. Once untouchables, they are now seen as important members of the community and their children are increasingly well-educated." This is another case not so much about ignorance *per se*, but one in which two cultures interacted and influenced each other not because of calculated intent but simply by learning from each other, through the process of living and working together over long periods of time, about different ways to live. It is globalization in action.

This kind of change helps explain what happened when Mac Odell returned to Dhankuta with his wife, sister, and brother-in-law, 32 years after he left it. When he made known at a local hotel that he used to teach in Dhankuta, the man behind the counter jumped to his feet and said, "Are you Mac Odell? I was in your 5th grade class!" He then took the party on a tour of the town, starting with one of Mac's fellow teachers at the high school where they had both taught over 30 years before. They were invited inside, taken to a lovely balcony overlooking the valley, and served a delicious meal of fried rice and omelet. The host sat with them part of the time, fussed over them, and made sure everything was perfect (this is all standard Nepalese hospitality).

Mac recalled that when he first arrived in Dhankuta in 1962 no one would go beyond politely talking with him, and he was almost never invited into anyone's house the entire time he was there. Even when he invited people to his house no one would eat with him or in his presence—in terms of the all-important realm of sharing food, he was considered an "untouchable," but now he and his family were being treated like honored guests. During the meal Mac's student had rounded up other old teachers and students, and they went on through the town like the Pied Piper, collecting more people at each stop, sitting and reminiscing. When it got dark, the guide went to a friend who opened his store and loaned them several flashlights, as the party proceeded into the night, from house to house, a small parade of excited friends, former students, and now their children, as Mac was greeted like a long lost hero. Later they went to Mac's old school, now coeducational, with a female headmistress who warmly welcomed them, clearly aware of how much these western volunteers had made her future possible.

I imagine similar receptions would await other Volunteers if they returned to the towns and villages they lived and worked in. Most Volunteers came to love the people they worked with, and, from the few cases we can document, the Nepalis mostly returned those sentiments. Nor would such instances of Nepalese hospitality be limited to Peace Corps Volunteers. I mention such examples only because I'm more aware of them.

When I returned in 2011 after a 42-year absence to Dolpa District, where I had done Ph.D. research, the welcome was overwhelming, even though few people that I had known were still alive, and the overwhelming majority of the village had not been born (or were too young to remember) when I lived there. In this case the reception was due not to living memories of my presence, which few would have possessed, but to extravagant and greatly overstated rumors and myths about me (for example, that I had lived in the village for six years, rather than the one year I was actually there, or that my son had been born in the village, instead of in the hospital in Kathmandu) that had proliferated over the years.

Without roads or electricity (although even in this remote area there were a few cell phones by 2011), there is little that city folks would call "entertainment" available to people living in the middle of Dolpa. Activities they could enjoy during their down time after long grueling days working in the millet and buckwheat fields or engaging in long distance trading trips were mostly limited to socializing with family and friends. Perhaps one diversion, not only available but also cheap, was telling tales, which grew taller over the years, about the rather anomalous foreigner (there were virtually no other non-nationals in Dolpa in the late 1960s) who had lived among them once upon a time.

6

GLOBALIZING IN THE U.S.

The Return

A period of time such as that experienced during a Peace Corps assignment is a little like the production of a play. It occurs in stages: preparation and rehearsal, setting the stage, a plot with its various twists and turns, and a conclusion. The conclusion can be uplifting or gloomy, depending on how the plot plays out and the expectations of the audience.

The conclusion of our Peace Corps term of service in Nepal took place two years after training at George Washington University began (the commitment was for 24 months, including training). A language expert from the State Department came out from Washington to test our knowledge of Nepali. It was a moment of truth for some: as we were each waiting our turn to be tested, one Volunteer anxiously asked me how to say, in Nepali: "I can't say that in Nepali." As was frequently the case from the beginning of training, and during the entire time in Nepal, this was an occasion of exhaustive and exhausting conferences, discussions, and filling out of questionnaires, in this case about the entire, beginning-to-end Peace Corps experience.

The whole process was somewhat anti-climactic. As the end of our time in Nepal edged inexorably nearer, we began to think ahead more than ponder whatever was the job at hand. Amid the goodbyes and farewells were thoughts of: What next? Specifically, how would we get home? Half the world to traverse back to the U.S—regardless of which direction we chose—was an invitation to more routes home than could be imagined. If we wanted to see the world mostly if not entirely on the U.S. government dime, this was our chance.

Pandemonium reigned in the Peace Corps hostel, which was crowded with people packing, and every available place filled with trunks and boxes. As Mike Frame wrote in a letter home, "It is really hard to believe that my term here is almost over with and that it's time to think about coming home. Coming back to the over-developed world of automation and communication, where time is counted in seconds and not in days is rather frightening to think about. Sometimes we sit around and laugh about how out-of-place we are going to feel when we get home."[42]

We also began thinking, with some apprehension, about what would await us when we did return. What had happened to our families and friends and romantic interests over these two years? For that matter, what had happened to our country? We departed from it so optimistically situated: imbued with the energetic promise of the New Frontier, a land full of potential and possibility, which, even if we felt we had failed to do all we had hoped to do in Nepal, at some level we ourselves personified, or hoped we did.

In the meantime, the man who had urged us to ask not what our country could do for us but what we could do for our country, lay buried in Arlington Cemetery, slain by a bullet whose ultimate provenance was still being passionately debated. The assassination reduced us to despair, and at the time I wrote a letter home which mentioned this: "In my headier moments I find myself imagining Nepal as a sort of Asian Oz, with the King the wizard and Kathmandu the Emerald City. An unabashedly Romantic view, perhaps, but one needs sporadic forays into fantasy to preserve morale from the corrosion of despair. From a vantage point of 12,000 miles, the U.S. sometimes becomes the best of all possible worlds. But during the weeping week before Thanksgiving, the miasma emanating from those foreign shores forced me to wonder what kind of country I am representing." It's fair to say that our reactions were much like those of our stateside countrymen, except that our sense of loss was accentuated by being so far from the land and people we were trying to represent.

What would be our fate, and that of the Peace Corps, now? Our country was still at peace, but already rumors were circulating that USAID in Bangkok was looking for people interested in doing village-level work in Vietnam. What experience could better prepare someone for that kind of a job than two years spent in a rural Asian country as a Peace Corps Volunteer? Several Nepal I Volunteers ended up in Vietnam, in one capacity or another, over the next few years.

In any case, 52 Volunteers filled out the questionnaires (although not every Volunteer answered every question), while 53 participated in the discussions (one Volunteer arrived a day late). In addition to the eight Volunteers who terminated early, nine Volunteers (including me), were unable to attend the conference.

In my case, Sir Edmund Hillary had just begun a program of helping the Sherpas, with whom he had been climbing for so many years, lead better and more promising lives. He felt he owed them something, and asked them what he could do. They said they wanted schools for their children, "who have eyes, but still they are blind," as they wrote in a petition which they presented to him. Since by this time I had two years of experience in Nepalese education under my belt, I wrote Sir Edmund to tell him that I thought I might be of some use in the school-building program he had just launched in villages in the Mt. Everest region.

His quick reaction (his rapid response and decisiveness were always like this when a command decision was required) was that this all seemed to make eminent sense, with the result that I spent three months working with Sherpa teachers who were already there, and helping set things up with Sherpa communities to build still more schools. Then I spent another three months as a member of the Himalayan Schoolhouse Expedition of 1964, during which we built three schools (in Namche Bazaar, Chaunrikharka, and Junbesi), two bridges at the bottom of the Namche hill, a water-collecting tank in Khumjung, and an airstrip at Lukla, in addition to making the first ascent of Thamserku. [43]

One of the great pleasures of that expedition was working with Ed Hillary, whom I came to admire enormously. What was most impressive to me was that he treated everyone exactly the same, whether it was the King of Nepal, the Queen of England, an impoverished Sherpa, or me. Trekking with him, and sometimes sharing a tent with him, resulted in many wonderful and enlightening conversations about everything from the needs of Sherpas to how Tenzing Norgay had been as a climbing partner on Everest, including details that he would not put into print (a sense of confidentiality I will continue to respect here).

Naturally this entire project was an exciting opportunity for me, but also, or so I thought, for the Peace Corps in Nepal. Some Peace Corps staff agreed with me, while others thought working with Sherpa communities as a member of an expedition led by Sir Edmund Hillary did not fit the conventional Peace Corps mold of teacher in a village school. I had met similar resistance when I wanted to live with a Brahmin family in Kathmandu in order to improve my faltering Nepali, at a time when no one had ever done such a thing. The Peace Corps doctor cautioned against it, for health reasons. In that case, as in the Hillary one, the Peace Corps was both timid and beginning to become encrusted in its own bureaucratic ways—perhaps an inevitable course of events in any large government establishment. One cannot be imaginative, innovative, and bold forever—eventually established routines take over.

Two specialists were brought in from Washington to conduct the final evaluation. The following discussion of the conference and questionnaire results is based on a document, "Completion of Service Conference," produced by the two evaluators, Dr. Harold Morris and Mr. E. Robert Hellawell.

The final evaluation process was accepted rather passively by Volunteers, the authors wrote. Volunteers cooperated, but without great enthusiasm or emotion. Several felt that they had already gone over the topics many times, and that there was little left to say that had not already been said. They were apparently suffering, and not without reason, from evaluation fatigue. Perhaps the Peace

Corps had already succumbed to the bureaucratic insistence on massive documentation of even the obvious, so that no one could be blamed for lack of data if requested by some congressional investigation or other.

Despite our weariness with the whole process, the majority agreed on two major points. The gloomy one was the widespread perception of lack of concrete accomplishment in their jobs. The uplifting one is that two years in the Peace Corps had been a more maturing experience than any other two-year experience they had had or could even imagine having. Forty-eight (of the 52) were moderately to very satisfied with the way things had turned out, and only four said they were not satisfied. Forty-two felt that their understanding of the place of the U.S. in the world had increased, while 10 felt no such change in understanding. Overall, asked to consider how well they had done as Volunteers, taking into account not only their work, but also meeting host country nationals and learning about Nepal as well as giving some sense of what America is like, 51 felt they had done moderately to very well, and only one felt he or she had not done well at all.

I was not able to determine definitively why this one naysayer had such a negative perception of accomplishment, or why four were not satisfied by the experience. Simply through bad luck, some Volunteers ended up in unusually difficult job conditions or house-mate assignments, or both. Sometimes these situations could be more or less happily resolved, but not always. Such cases remind us that this book tends to accentuate the positive, partly because those who left early, including so-called failures, had disappeared somewhere into the nation (if not the world), and I was unable to contact them. It is also the case that the single doubter might have a dramatically different view now, 50 years later, than he or she did at the time, but about that we will never know.

Most (45 yes, seven no) thought they had made a contribution to the country, although most felt this was true only in a general way, and it was difficult to point to specific accomplishments. They felt that health, difficulties with language, and lack of effective working counterparts interfered with giving all they could to their work. The overwhelming majority felt much personal satisfaction and growth as a result of their Peace Corps experience. They stressed their freedom to be an individual as the source of their greatest satisfaction and hoped this freedom could accompany any future expansion of the Peace Corps.

Asked about career goals before and after joining the Peace Corps, about one third reported no change, while two thirds reported that as a result of their Peace Corps experience, they wanted to pursue a teaching career or a career in international affairs. Even those who reported no change for the most part emphasized different aspects of their previous interests. Most felt an increased interest in international affairs, more certainty about future personal goals, and greater maturity and more tolerance of cultural differences as a result of their two years in Nepal.

Volunteers were very "action oriented," and what negativity they did express concerned the lack of tangible results from their jobs. They attributed this in part to their training, feeling that much of it was superfluous and some of it downright misleading. They felt there should have been more instruction in specific job skills, or else selection of Volunteers who had already achieved a higher level of such skills. Volunteers seemed more critical of training at the end of two years in Nepal than they did 40 or more years later. Interestingly, the one issue about which the most feeling was expressed was not directly related to their situations on the ground, and over which they had no control: that local Peace Corps staff not use the helicopter to make visits to them in the field, since this was contrary to the Peace Corps image they had tried so hard to project.

Shortly after the conference Volunteers began leaving for home, but in almost all cases by very lengthy and indirect routes. Most Volunteers elected to take the cash equivalent of a return plane ticket, and to stretch that as far as it would go in travel to various destinations, some of it overland. Some started in Thailand and travelled to Japan or Indonesia or through the south Pacific. Others went to India, thence to the

Soviet Union and eastern Europe, or through Afghanistan, Iran, and Mediterranean and north African countries to Europe. These trips lasted in some cases for as long as six or seven months. Clearly, the Peace Corps experience in Nepal had only whetted the Volunteers' appetite for international travel and experience, not satisfied it.

Education

Most Volunteers were of roughly college age when they joined the Peace Corps in 1962—either fresh B.A.'s, or without a B.A. but with some college under their belt. At the conclusion of their time in Nepal only five were over 30 years of age. Many RPCVs (Returned Peace Corps Volunteers) elected to continue their education. But they did so not just because they were of the age when that sort of thing is expected, but because their Peace Corps experience had fundamentally reoriented what they perceived to be their future educational needs and expectations.

Before enlisting in the Peace Corps they had, for the most part, pursued educational goals more or less because that was the established routine for Americans of their age and class. And as was typical of many other Americans in the same situation then, some of them had grown tired or restless with the educational experience they were undergoing. Several spoke of feeling burned out. They may have been convinced of the ultimate need and importance of more education, but they found the process lacking in excitement and motivation. They were hungry for something different, and whatever else it was, the Peace Corps certainly offered something different.

The Peace Corps experience transformed that passive attitude. After two years in Nepal, many of the Volunteers came back to pursue education with a vengeance. If they had only graduated from high school, they headed for college. If they had attended college but not received their baccalaureate degrees, they went back to finish, often with changed majors or academic focus. If they already had

B.A.'s, they pursued advanced degrees. If they already had master's degrees, they pursued doctorates, or bent their academic qualifications in new employment directions.

Returning to the U.S. to pursue educational goals required thinking ahead while they were still in Nepal. Getting accurate information from various institutions and sending off applications to some of them, via a postal system that was slow and, more important, unreliable, made for difficult and uncertain communication. For all practical purposes telephone transmission between Nepal and the United States did not exist in the early 1960s, and email and the Internet had not yet been dreamed of, let alone invented. The end results were sometimes different from what they might have been if applicants had submitted applications from the United States.

George Peck filled out Indian aerograms on an IBM Selectric typewriter (a state of the art typewriter at the time), writing "I am currently in the Peace Corps in Nepal. I have a B.S. degree from the University of Colorado, and I would like to apply for admission to your school." His first choice was biophysics at the University of Michigan. As a fallback, he also applied to the University of Idaho. Michigan replied that he would have to take an English proficiency test, have a sponsor in the U.S., and other similarly inappropriate and irritating requirements. Idaho replied with the offer of a teaching assistantship. So George went to Idaho.

The group of 70 who survived training and went to Nepal included 46 who had received B.A. degrees, and 12 who had attended college, and in some cases had acquired A.A. (Associate of Arts) degrees or specialized diplomas. Seven had received M.A.'s, while five had graduated from high school with no further educational training. There were no Ph.D.'s in the group.

Over the 25 years or so following the end of their Peace Corps service, most of the returned Volunteers acquired more academic credentials, regardless of their previous level of education. Fifteen received B.A. degrees. Thirty-seven received master's degrees, while 15 received doctoral degrees: 14 were awarded a Ph.D., and one an Ed.D. Two people earned divinity degrees, and one received a law degree. Altogether 44 people received a total of 66 college degrees after they returned. Of the five who had not attended college at all before Peace Corps, three went on to receive B.A.'s; the other two never attended college but did acquire specialized vocational credentials.

The Ph.D. degrees were awarded in anthropology (three), rural sociology (one), geophysics (one), sociology (one), urban planning (one), political science (one), public administration (one), physics (one), agricultural economics (one), education (one), education and program evaluation (one), and biochemistry (one). In some cases these represented a continuation of previous interests (anthropology, physics, geophysics, agricultural economics, biochemistry). Other academic interests developed out of the Nepal experiences and were entirely new fields for those studying them.

The three anthropologists (of whom I am one) comprise a case in point. Two of them had scarcely heard of anthropology before going to Nepal. Bob Rhoades had grown up on a farm in the middle of the flatness of Oklahoma and was working on a B.A. in agriculture when he went to Nepal. He worked in agricultural extension, but immediately he could see that the rigid American models he'd known and been taught and practiced all his life weren't working there. He was amazed at the vertical nature of Nepalese life in general and of the verticality of Nepalese agriculture in particular. That converted his whole approach away from technology and towards wanting to understand why Nepali farmers did what they did. He concluded that they were rational actors in their own context. He ended up with a Ph.D. in ecological anthropology. He spent 10 years in highland Peru and became a leading authority on the potato. Later he became chair of the anthropology department at the University of Georgia. His whole point of view and professional career were informed by his experience in Nepal.

Peter Prindle was in the process of finishing his first year of medical school when he applied to the Peace Corps and ended up in Nepal. His switch to anthropology from medicine was a far-reaching one; he eventually published a book on the Brahmin village in east Nepal he had studied for his degree.

I had discovered the existence of anthropology during my senior year in college. What I did not realize then was that Nepal would become my focus and that I would spend the rest of my life involved in Himalayan studies. Although during the depths of bitterly cold Minnesota winters, in my 38 years at Carleton College, I sometimes contemplated changing my geographic concentration to the South Pacific, I never did so. By that time Nepal (and later Bhutan) had become like a second home to me, and I could not tear myself away from it all. I had so many friends in Nepal by this time, social and professional, that much of what I found meaningful and satisfying in life was involved with them. I spent two years as a Fulbright Scholar helping found the Department of Sociology and Anthropology at Tribhuvan University, and then in 2009 did something similar, helping start Royal Thimphu College, the first private college in Bhutan.

In 1962 there were, incontestably, three Himalayan Kingdoms: Nepal, Sikkim, and Bhutan. Sikkim was swallowed by India in 1974, leaving two, and then Nepal's Hindu monarchy imploded in 2006. That left Bhutan, the ultimate, but elusive, Himalayan goal, a kind of miniature Nepal, governed by a monarchy (Buddhist, not Hindu, which made it the only predominantly Tibetan Buddhist country in the world), and the one untouched country we Himalayanists wanted to enter. I had been trying to get to Bhutan for 45 years, so I felt it was about time.

Carleton gave me the opportunity to play a formative role in the development of South Asian studies there. Among other projects, they gave me time to go to Nepal to conduct research on the Sherpas I had worked with during the Hillary expedition, and to publish a book on them, and also to research and write a book on the history of democracy in Nepal. My Ph.D. research, on Sahar Tara village in Dolpa District, also came out as a book while I was at Carleton.

Like the Ph.D. degrees, the M.A. degrees were all over the academic map, but they tended for the most part to be in fields with obvious links to problem-solving in the social, political, and economic world: economics, education, agricultural economics, South Asian studies, industrial arts, family counseling, social work, plant pathology, business and public administration, animal sciences, public administration and political science, parasitology, police administration, food and nutrition, and public health.

The knowledge gained from studying these fields enriched and enlarged the Volunteers' abilities to apply skills they had either utilized or discovered for the first time in Nepal. It is also true that recruiting Volunteers to these disciplines enriched the stock of human capital in these fields with people who brought two years of overseas field experience to bear on them. Over time, as these and other Volunteers returned to the U.S., the shape of these fields began to reflect the values and abilities and experiences of those in them. Returned Volunteers played a part in reformulating the disciplines they had studied as graduate students.

Occupations

Forty-four Volunteers receiving degrees after their time in Nepal meant new vocational directions for those receiving them. Those who had been adrift—personally or academically—were now motivated to seek work that would utilize their new-found skills. Perhaps the most frequent and innovative orientation was towards working in the international world. People who had never travelled abroad, or those who had barely been off the farms they grew up on, or had never flown in an airplane, now were working all over the world, mostly in Asia, Latin America, and Africa. Of the 70, 30 eventually settled into international work of some kind or other for the rest of their working lives: 14 of those returned to Nepal in various kinds of jobs and consultancies, and another 16 worked in dozens of other countries.

The most striking characteristics of the vocational directions Volunteers took are their variety and multiplicity.

Not only are there many different kinds of professions represented, but with very few exceptions, and in common with much of the American labor force during the latter decades of the 20th century, Volunteers moved from one occupation to another. Rather than stick with a single employer or type of job, most tried their hands at a variety of fields, either because they appealed to their changing interests, or because better opportunities presented themselves.

However, as Vietnam began to become a hot spot, which it did soon after our two years in Nepal were up, and the Army began increasing the size of its draft, occupational choice was no longer the wide open field it had been. Rich Emde is a good example of the kind of occupational hop-scotching that resulted. Rich came back home and was promptly drafted into the Army. He was trained as a helicopter mechanic and went to Vietnam for nine months. Then he went back to college full time, but he also started a janitorial business, which eventually became a business renting compact refrigerators. He dealt in real estate for a while, and then decided to pursue a career in product design, which he'd been trained to do. He and his wife went to Seattle, where there was "no snow, no mosquitoes, no tornadoes, and the pace of life was not as frenetic as Los Angeles and not as crowded as on the east coast.

"I bought a silly book called *What Color is Your Parachute?*, a sort of job search book. That made me think, wait a minute, what I've always done or what I've always enjoyed doing is what this book says I should do. So, I said I really like to talk to people and educate and kind of be the expert and then be done with it and move on and do it again. What I've really done in the past and enjoyed doing was talking to people. So, I started doing some informational interviews, talking to people that ran tour programs. I went to the state capital where I saw this fellow who had just started the daily tour program. I wanted to ask him how he did it, how he liked it, and all the questions you ask, and then I asked, why isn't the capital open on weekends? And he said, 'You want a job?'

"And I've been here ever since. So, the medical career

went out with the first biology course, the design career went out when I found out what color my parachute was, and here I am. I don't know what my next one's gonna be, but I'm sure the Nepal experience will have some effect on what I do."

Ken Van Sickle's case was similarly full of pursuing a variety of different fields. When his Peace Corps time was up Ken flew to Bangkok, where he heard there were counter-insurgency positions open in Vietnam. He flew on to Saigon, applied for one of the positions, and was accepted. He went back to the U.S. for a break before training, during which time they lost his papers, so he went back to college, this time at the University of Oklahoma, for two semesters. He got married and was about to be drafted, so he volunteered for the Navy as a hospital foreman. Three months later he was on an aircraft carrier near the Philippines, and then spent some time in San Diego before spending a year in Vietnam, during the Tet offensive, when he worked in emergency medicine. Then he lived in San Diego for two more years.

By the 1970s he and his family headed back to North Dakota, where he resumed schooling at the University of North Dakota at Grand Forks and got a B.A. degree in zoology. He took exams to go on to medical school but then decided he was getting a little old for that, so he started graduate school in parasitology, mostly doing research, and received an M.A. in that field.

That was a time when jobs became scarce because the government shut down all the hiring it was doing in this line of work, so he left school to work for a big farming corporation, where he took over the irrigation section. Then he opened a branch office for a dealer in irrigation pivots; within six months the dealer had gone bankrupt, so Ken started his own pivot dealership which he ran for nine years in South Dakota. Jimmy Carter killed the big water project in South Dakota that he depended on, so next he went to work for a manufacturing plant and was transferred to Kansas.

Remembering how much he liked Colorado during Peace Corps training, he returned and got a job with Coors brewery, where he stayed for three years. After that he decided to get back on his own and bought a tanning salon which he ran for another nine years, till he got tired of all the hours and got certified as a welder and became shop foreman at a manufacturing plant there, building steel rock splitters.

A more geographically confined case is that of Les Gile. After working as an agronomist in agricultural extension in Pokhara, Les returned to New England where he taught for a while in high school, spent two years in milk inspection for the state of Massachusetts, seven years managing a farm, four years in carpentry building homes, and finally seven years in the mental health field before retiring.

Some Volunteers followed professions that they had not even heard of before they went to Nepal. Flemming Heegaard said he "had a career in the last 38 years mixed between academic teaching and consulting and international development. I have sort of stuck with the international development, and I would never have done that without the Peace Corps, because I didn't know that international development existed before I joined the Peace Corps."

Six Volunteers found themselves back in Nepal within a year of leaving it.

Mac and Barbara returned to a Sherpa village in east Nepal for a second assignment, to work out their ideas on education in rural Nepal. Their story is told at the end of the following chapter.

Within six months of our termination Bob Murphy was back in Nepal with the Tom Dooley Foundation conducting a national health survey covering about 300,000 people. After a couple of years of that he managed a high-end resort in the Tarai called Tiger Tops, which offered the opportunity to see wildlife (such as rhinos and deer, and, very rarely, tigers) while riding elephants through the Tarai jungles.

After four years at Tiger Tops Bob moved on to a series of international development jobs over the next almost 50 years, mostly with AID or funded by AID. The list of countries in which he has worked is the longest of any of those in Nepal I who later worked in international development: Nepal, Peru, Sri Lanka, Honduras, Morocco,

Haiti, Nicaragua, Guatemala, Panama, Columbia, Bolivia, El Salvador, Bosnia Herzegovina, Croatia, Italy, East Timor, Venezuela, Costa Rica, Ecuador, India, Bangladesh, Bulgaria, Angola, Pakistan, Hungary, Iraq, Afghanistan, and Albania.

After working his own farm in east Nepal during a second stint as a Volunteer, Mike Frame worked for the Peace Corps in Nepal for five years, as its agricultural staff member, USAID in Nepal for two more years, again as agricultural staff, taking time out in the middle of it all to help organize and build an agricultural cooperative farm in western Wisconsin. He ended up going back to Nepal and opening restaurants in Kathmandu ("Mike's Breakfast" became known internationally and is still a beacon for expats there) and Hotel Phewa in Pokhara, after Kathmandu got too crowded for him.

Dorothy Mierow did not return to Nepal within six months, but she did spend most of the rest of her life in Nepal. She served three terms as a Peace Corps Volunteer, then worked as a geographer in a variety of jobs in Nepal and Bhutan, making maps for the U.N. and other agencies, and publishing several books on the birds, trees, and flowers of Nepal. Her main project was to build the Natural History Museum in Pokhara, an extensive collection of butterflies, insects, birds, and models of wildlife found in the Annapurna region. She formally adopted some of the children in a Gurung family, and died of cancer weeks before the 38th reunion of Nepal I in Nepal in 2000.

Finally, after a lengthy trip home through the Soviet Union and other European countries, Jerry Young returned to Nepal as a member of the Peace Corps staff in Kathmandu, the first former PCV to do so. He later went on to a career in public health both internationally (including Nepal) and in Wisconsin.

The professional lives of many Volunteers were influenced by their time in Nepal, but not necessarily in obvious or consistent ways. After his Peace Corps tour in Nepal, Bert Puchtler went to Laos for five years to work in rural development with USAID. Because Pathet Lao

(Communist) forces controlled the roads, he had to fly once a week from his home and family in the capital city, Vientiane, to his rural post. He was demoralized when, towards the end of his five-year assignment, he was told to forget about rural development and concentrate on what later came to be called "the secret war," so called because the American bombings and American-supported counter-insurgency operations there and in Cambodia were not generally reported in the American press. Bert's case, and those of other Volunteers who ended up in Vietnam, illustrate the narrow line separating Peace Corps experience from recruitment or being drafted into active involvement in armed conflicts. Bert subsequently left Laos and spent the rest of his working life employed by the federal Indian Health Service in Alaska.

Some Volunteers went in entirely different directions after they returned from Nepal. After his return Paul Ahrens, trained originally as an engineer, wrote technical manuals for appliances (like toasters) to pay the rent, but his main interests were literary. He wrote poetry (as did others), and he also wrote plays, some of which were performed off-Broadway in New York. Nick Cibrario's ambitions of becoming a Catholic priest did not last long after enrolling in a Jesuit seminary. Instead, he became a high school teacher and, after retirement, a novelist (including, as of this writing, four published novels set in Nepal).

Dave Sears also ended up in an entirely different field. He had grown up on a farm and never wanted to be anything but a farmer. When he returned from Nepal he finished his college work with a B.A. in sociology, and from there he went on to an M.A. in guidance and counseling. He worked in government programs for the economically disadvantaged, but eventually returned to his first love, farming. He owned and operated a dairy farm in Missouri.

But through his church work he eventually entered a seminary in 1989 at age 48. He served as a lay pastor in rural Missouri towns while attending St. Paul School of Theology in Kansas City, Missouri, after which he served various congregations around the state. His Peace Corps experience totally reoriented his life, in that it made him realize, however belatedly, that he needed to focus on what was really important to him—the spiritual dimension of life.

Prior to serving in the Peace Corps Larry Wolfe had been a communications specialist in the Air Force, simultaneously enrolling part time in a local college as a sort of avocation. He finished college after his return from Nepal and went on for a master's and finally an Ed.D. degree, focusing on the administration of higher education. Indiana University offered him a job as director of records information. It was a commuter campus with 6,000 students. "I was there seven years, after which I went to a neighboring city, Hammond, and worked in educational planning for the city there for seven years. In the meantime I got my real estate broker's license. And I bought some apartment buildings, owned and operated a flower shop and also a bookstore, before retiring."

On the other hand, Bernie Snoyer came home to pursue wood carving, a skill he had practiced before entering the Peace Corps. He developed a career through work in interior design for bars, restaurants, and private homes, and he ran his own cabinet shop. Finally he and his wife bought an old mansion in western Michigan, remodeled it, and converted it into a bed-and-breakfast.

The professional lives of some were more obviously affected by their Peace Corps experience, and to some degree extended that experience. Lee Tuveson's career was profoundly and explicitly affected by his time in Nepal. He reports, "I came home from the Peace Corps, much to the shivering delight of my parents who thought—especially my dad thought—that I was finally going to go to work and do something useful, which to his mind was the business world or something of that nature. Instead I went into the Foreign Service. He could never understand why I wanted to do that. But I realized that the Peace Corps really did give me a different perspective on the world—certainly different from that of any of my family and friends where I grew up. They never understood my motivation or my need to go back to the international arena and experience that again, to be in touch with other cultures.

"There's not one event that I can take from the whole experience and say it was this in itself that was unique. The treks, our leaders like Willi Unsoeld, my friends—the totality of it was unique. My friend Jim [his reference is to the current author] left me with the inquisitiveness about the world we live in, because he had an interest in understanding why things were going on, what the behaviors were, and he already had his anthropological bent, already it was working in those days. I remember our conversations and his observations of what was going on in Bhaktapur. His interest and observations of the world we were living in were very instructive because they gave me a perspective on a lot of the things that were going on. He was already beginning to put this together, in his own mind in any case, as to what all of this meant. The *pujas*, the cycle of events, the Dasain festival—Jim as a housemate was very interested in understanding what that was. Those associations with individual Volunteers as well as the totality of the experience are what were rewarding about the whole experience.

"When I went into the Foreign Service I had an opportunity to go with the State Department and be a visa stamper in the consular section, or to go with USIA and engage in public diplomacy. What I hoped and assumed would happen when I went with USIA is that it would be a continuation of the Peace Corps experience. That was what I wanted—to be involved in people-to-people diplomacy. The USIA job was called a Student Affairs Officer, in Guayaquil, Ecuador. So that's what I decided to do.

"The Foreign Service was disappointing in many ways, but it met one level of my expectations in that I did have a lot of contact with the people (one of whom became my wife) where I was assigned. I was not required to live in the consulate with other Americans. I was expected to live in the city in an apartment open to students from the university. My role was to engage student leaders in dialogue about the U.S. and our culture, and to impart to them those aspects of American life and foreign policy that were defensible.

"What was not satisfying was the bureaucratic structure,

the pecking order. I didn't realize the extent it impacted day-to-day work doing this kind of public diplomacy. I don't regret the Foreign Service experience, but I did not stay with it for more than five years, and then I left it and went into the civil service, so I did stay with the federal government. All this resulted in a kind of unintended career, because I went into personnel work thinking that it was another kind of person-to-person diplomacy, if you will. But working in personnel, recruitment, and whatever it turned out to be, looking back on 30 years in the civil service, it was all very bureaucratic.

"I suppose if I had it to do over again, and you never know, but maybe I was cut out to be some kind of a missionary, or better yet do what some of my Peace Corps friends have done, who have gone into international consulting. In fact, after I retired from the federal civil service in 1996, Flemming Heegaard told me of an opportunity in Tanzania. I hadn't been overseas in 25 years, but I did go as a consultant to Tanzania. What came out of that experience was the realization that my previous experience of 30 years ago was very meaningful because it gave me an ability to adapt to very different conditions.

"I also went to Palestine for two weeks, but those were very different experiences from anything I had done since the Peace Corps. That I could successfully adapt again to those societies says a lot about the Peace Corps experience. The flexibility, the adaptability, the ability to take care of yourself in circumstances that are so extraordinarily foreign—again, the Peace Corps experience was valuable in giving me a way to do all that." Lee's experience working for USIA was echoed by others who worked for the agency, such as Bob Proctor.

When Glenda returned home, her first job was teaching at a junior high school in Independence, Missouri. It was part of the Kansas City School District. They were under pressure to integrate their schools, and, as its first non-white teacher, she integrated hers. "I think when they looked at my background, they felt that I would be able to make that transition smoothly and that it would be easier for the school and for me, because I had that Peace Corps experience.

Another thing is that I left there and went to teach food and nutrition at my alma mater [Langston University, in Oklahoma]. When I was getting my master's degree in food and nutrition, they waived the requirement for my course in cultural food patterns (I think that was the name of it), because of my experiences in the Peace Corps."

Of course, some Volunteers who received doctoral degrees spent most of their working lives in higher education. Rather than remain members of the academy, though, eight of the 15 Volunteers who earned doctorates pursued careers outside of higher education.

After Mac Odell reenlisted for a second tour with the Peace Corps in Nepal, he returned to the U.S. to earn a Ph.D. at Cornell in rural sociology, with a development emphasis, and then worked in a variety of mostly short-term jobs in Pakistan, plus five years in Botswana before going back to Nepal for several years to help establish a new National Park at the base of Mt. Makalu in east Nepal. He also worked for Habitat for Humanity in Nepal, India, and Sri Lanka. A series of jobs and consultancies took him to Tanzania, Palestine, Egypt, Kenya, Malawi, Sierra Leone, Sudan, Jamaica, and Haiti doing grass-roots rural development work (which continues as of this writing), all built on what he learned during four years as a Peace Corps Volunteer in Nepal.

Dan Pierce enrolled at Wesleyan University for an M.S. in physics before returning to his alma mater, Stanford, for his Ph.D. in applied physics. After four years with the Federal Institute of Technology in Zurich, he settled down at the National Institute of Standards and Technology (formerly the National Bureau of Standards), near Washington, doing experimental physics research on electronic and magnetic properties of surfaces, interfaces, and thin films. He says his time in Nepal made him much more aware of cultural differences even in relatively similar countries like Germany and Switzerland.

Mark Schroeder earned his Ph.D. in agricultural economics at Cornell, with a dissertation on the impact of the new road from Kathmandu to Pokhara. He returned to Vermont and worked part-time for a building supply business, and the rest of the time farming, logging, sugaring, and raising beef. He also worked in the planning office for the state of Vermont.

Six of the Volunteers with Ph.D.'s became part of the standard American professoriate, but their teaching and research interests developed over time as academic departments and disciplines changed. The sociologist (Carl Jorgensen) and the three anthropologists (Bob Rhoades, Peter Prindle, and I) became involved, in addition to our core disciplines, in what came to be called, variously, cross-cultural studies, Asian studies, ethnic studies, and race relations. The biologist, Dave Towle, specialized in marine biology. Ralph Hambrick, with a Ph.D. in public administration, similarly followed the expanding branches of his discipline.

Such a broad spectrum of vocations and jobs makes it difficult to generalize about the kind of work Nepal I RPCVs have pursued, save that it is highly various. Nevertheless two threads might be identified that fairly consistently run through these examples. One is the tendency to be employed in jobs that are, loosely conceived, people-oriented. RPCVs are more likely to be out and about in field situations, dealing with people, than to be ensconced in a cubicle or office somewhere. The second tendency is to be in positions that require a fair amount of initiative and innovation to deal with changing circumstances. The RPCVs from Nepal I are generally not found in jobs in which they are required to follow rigid, inflexible, bureaucratic rules. Or if they are, they chafe under them.

More importantly, Volunteers moved up in class. Those who came from less privileged backgrounds, who had limited access to education and travel, and who had uncertain prospects in the pursuit of higher educational credentials, were now sprung loose. They saw visions of what could be and pursued them. As a result, they held jobs at higher levels in organizations they could have scarcely dreamed of before. Those who came from higher-income backgrounds built on them and went still higher. Following the general demographic trends of the United States during this period, class mobility among Nepal I RPCVs was universally upwards.

Of the 70 Volunteers who went to Nepal in 1962, 39 returned to Nepal at least once in the ensuing years, some just to visit their old haunts, others to work or do research; among those who attended the reunion in 2000 in Pokhara were several who had not returned until then. All but one of those who had not returned to Nepal expressed a strong interest in going back, and some were making active plans to do so.

One interesting statistic worth noting is that from the end of service in 1964 until 2008, there was always at least one Nepal I Volunteer living and working in Nepal. A less probable statistic is that the three Nepal I Volunteers who never left Nepal, whether physically (i.e., residing mostly in Nepal) or metaphysically (i.e., teaching and writing about Nepal, but mostly from American soil) all happened to be born and raised in, or a lifelong resident of, the same small southeastern Minnesota town—Northfield. They had not met or heard of each other prior to Peace Corps training.

Family Life

Gradually, but inexorably, the Volunteers got on with their lives through the rest of the 20th century, ascending the ladder of academic achievement, acquiring credentials, and joining the workforce in a variety of ways. Most also began to form families and produce the next generation. Of the 70 Volunteers, 60 married, including four couples who arrived at Peace Corps training already married.

Three more marriages of Nepal I Volunteers to each other took place in Nepal during the period of Peace Corps service. In addition, one Volunteer married an American working as a secretary in the Peace Corps office, and one Volunteer married an Indian residing in Nepal while he was a Volunteer. Two Volunteers married Marine guards stationed at the American Embassy in Kathmandu shortly after their tour of service was over. As mentioned before, Barbara, who was married and divorced before the Peace Corps, married a Nepali she met during her second tour of duty.

Thus in addition to the eight Volunteers married before they joined the Peace Corps, another 11 married someone they met as a result of their having been in Nepal. Of nine single women of marriageable age in the group, six married someone with a Nepal connection. In sum, 19 Volunteers were married to someone they met either before they went to Nepal or as a result of their having gone to Nepal in the Peace Corps. Finally, towards the end of their time in Nepal one more Volunteer couple announced their intention to marry, but the engagement was broken off.

Of all 60 Volunteers who married, including the woman who married and divorced before the Peace Corps, 23 divorced, and four of these divorced more than once. Two of the four couples who came to the Peace Corps already married subsequently divorced after returning to the U.S., and two of the three Volunteer couples who married in Nepal later divorced. Two of the four who, after returning to the U.S., married Nepal-related but non-Peace Corps spouses, also divorced. Sharing an interest in or experience of Nepal did not seem to be much of a guarantee of marital harmony or stability.

Of the 60 who married, 56 had a total of 124 children, either naturally or by adoption. Twenty-one of the 124 were produced from the all-Volunteer marriages. Of the 124 children, 78 were sons, 41 were daughters, and the sex of five is unknown. I know of no reason why the sexual ratio is so heavily skewed towards males, other than that with such a small sample, size variation of this order could be random. The "natural" sex ratio at birth is generally taken to be about 105 (105 boys to 100 girls).

One hundred five of the children were natural offspring, while 19 were adopted. At least six of the 19 were non-white—some African American, some Asian, some Latin American, and some mixtures of all of the above. Rolf and Julie Goetze didn't want to bring more than two children into the world, so they gave birth to two and then adopted two more, one of Asian ancestry, the other African American. Thus even in having families, the idealism underlying the

Peace Corps continued.

Cross-racial adoptions are no doubt common among American adoptions generally. Certainly the cross-racial adoptions found among Nepal I Volunteers are consistent with the common belief among Peace Corps folks, assumed even if not explicitly formulated, that the basic, essential, and critical core of all human beings is cultural or social, not racial or genetic. Two ancillary and unspoken assumptions seem to be operating here: the first is that race unnaturally divides human beings; the second is that culture does not necessarily unite us, but it can, and we should do everything we can to make it do so.

These explicit or implicit beliefs lay behind and corroborated the original decision of many Volunteers to go to a place like Nepal in the first place. Volunteers believed that anyone could go anywhere (remember that most Volunteers in Nepal I applied to the Peace Corps willing to go wherever they were assigned) and live with any type of people and establish the common, unifying human bond. Where such beliefs were absent or not held explicitly, simply because they had not been much thought about, living and working for two years in Nepal, alongside Nepalis from various walks of life, almost guaranteed coming to such conclusions.

Finding out more about the children—and grand-children—of these Volunteers would require another book. But anecdotally, it is my impression that although children of the Volunteers, to the extent that I know about them, have followed many widely different paths, and not all of them smooth ones (some have ended up estranged from their parents, or even in prison), they broadly share the commonality of having grown up in the shadow of their parents' experience in Nepal. If and when they meet, they recognize their affinities.

Many Volunteers have taken their children and spouses to Nepal, to show them the places they lived and the people they knew so many years before, all of which the children would have heard much about in the process of growing up. Some of the Volunteer children were born in Nepal while their parents were working or doing research there. My son was born in Nepal, and both my son and my daughter attended primary and secondary school there. When my daughter pursued graduate study in comparative literature, one of her languages was Sanskrit (the other two were Latin and Medieval English). Both have made return trips to Nepal independent of my own travels—the stamp is indelible. Some of the Volunteers' children have followed their parents' examples and joined the Peace Corps themselves, although none have gone to Nepal. Whether they avoided Nepal, or simply were not able to garner an assignment there (Nepal became and remained a highly competitive country until the Peace Corps ceased its operations there in 2004) is an interesting question I am unable to answer. Perhaps a partial answer will be available after the return of the Peace Corps Nepal in 2012. By that time the relevant examples will likely be grandchildren instead of children.

7

GLOBALIZATION:
THE NEPAL I EXPERIENCE

Globalization, like similar words of recent coinage, is a polyvalent term used in dramatically different ways, depending on whether one wants to promote or constrain it. Those who believe free markets advance prosperity and political freedom think globalization should be encouraged, while those who believe uncontrolled free markets produce overseas sweat shops and political repression see globalization as cruel, debasing, and exploitative. But at its non-ideological base, globalization is a process involving the flow of multifarious parts that sometimes work against each other in clashing "scapes" (ethnoscapes, fiancescapes, and so on; see Chapter One)—goods, services, capital, labor, images, information, ideas, and power. Contingent upon where one is in the system, these can simultaneously work for or against one's interests—it depends on whose ox is being gored.

These movements pass across continents and hemispheres, over land masses and oceans, through nation states and spheres of political influence, and penetrate ecological zones and cultural areas. Few humans on the planet escape its effects, regardless of where they live or, increasingly, where they are migrating. More and more, the movements of these flows are conducted and regulated through the medium of keys tapped on electronic keyboards, but ultimately they benefit or harm individuals.

Not only individuals, but nation-states, corporations, and international organizations are also actors on the globalization stage. They pursue sometimes agonistic and antagonistic ends. Prominent among these actors is the United States. For all its internal social and cultural diversity, the United States forms an entity that is seen by the rest of the world, at least, not as internally differentiated, but monolithic, with a unitary character, strength, and purpose. These qualities are not static, although they may seem that way from a distance. They change and drift and respond over time to pressures and influences from every corner of the globalizing globe.

Separated from the population centers of other continents (except South America) by vast oceans, the United States has lived most of its existence in blissful ignorance of the rest of the world. It has been a generally monolingual (English-speaking, after the first generation), mono-cultural (mostly Christian), and, especially in its political and economic power centers, mostly white country. Even though the demographic composition has dramatically changed with greatly increasing numbers of immigrants from non-European countries since the 1960s, the perception of the U.S. outside its borders is still largely stereotypical, based in part on the images seen in motion pictures, such as those starring Clint Eastwood, and on television programs, such as Bay Watch, the most popular television program in Sri Lanka. The U.S. has no experience of war with foreigners (as distinct from violent unrest among its own citizens, or terrorist attacks) on its own shores. Its wars have been fought in other countries when and where it thinks, sometimes mistakenly, its interests are best served and protected by such wars.

Since World War II, its overseas armies have been largely self-contained and self-sufficient, housed in concrete fortresses separated from the local population when not in battle with them. Army personnel as a whole have not known much about or interacted with local populations, with the obvious exceptions of clandestine operatives in Europe during World War II, or among counter-insurgency forces in Vietnam and Iraq. Of course, they have also married local women and brought them back to the U.S., continuing the ancient and well-established custom of invading or occupying armies. But such romantic attractions apart, and special exceptions notwithstanding, as a group American forces have not been expected to know much about local populations or to speak local languages. Generally speaking, that's been considered State Department turf.

American armed forces do make periodic well-intentioned attempts to win the "hearts and minds" of local populations with support for intensive language training, schooling in cultural sensitivity, cultivating relationships with villagers (including giving candy to children), and the like. Apart from such laudable efforts, the main rationale for the presence of armed forces in foreign lands is to exert military might. Whatever communication is required takes place primarily through that medium, up and down the chain of command. We expect high-ranking military counterparts in other countries to speak English; if they don't know English, we usually expect them to learn it. Training of military officers from other countries in the U.S. helps in this process.

One result of this self-contained presence is a rather insular, provincial, and self-absorbed American view of the world. Our knowledge of world history and geography is notoriously limited. One story, perhaps apocryphal, has it that an information telephone operator in the U.S., asked for the number of a party in New Mexico, replied that she did not have access to phone numbers in foreign countries.

A non-apocryphal story concerns one of the Nepal I Volunteers, David Kollasch, who returned from Nepal in the mid-1960s to his Iowa roots. Enrolled in a local university, he became good friends with a student from Africa. David was invited to a family wedding, where all the participants and guests were traditional, Midwestern German Catholics. When he brought his African friend with him as a guest, the wedding party was stunned. Everyone was polite about it, but it was apparent that meeting a coal black African was a first-in-a-lifetime experience for most of them.

David was surprised at their surprise. His experience in Nepal had so altered his frame of reference that he hadn't thought much about the African's place of origin, and even less about his appearance. David had been more deeply influenced by his time in Nepal than even he perhaps had realized. He had internalized ways of evaluating and dealing with people who looked and spoke differently from him, so much so that he was not aware of his own transformation. No doubt those in the wedding party were changed too, if only a little, by the whole occasion. They were not likely to be so taken aback the next time they met someone who looked so different from themselves.

This kind of experience has happened countless times as a result of the presence of returned Peace Corps Volunteers who have opened social, religious, and political doors in their communities across the country. The experiences of returned Nepal I Volunteers recounted below are specific to unique times and places. But there is no reason to doubt that most of the almost 4,000 subsequent Volunteers who lived and worked in Nepal, or the 200,000 other Volunteers who have served around the world, and then returned to the United States to tell the tale, have been altered in broadly similar ways.

But everything has become more complex now. As globalization has taken hold, later generations of Volunteers know more about Nepal before getting there, and Nepalis know more about Americans when they do come. Most Nepalis do not remember a time when the Peace Corps (and similar international organizations) was not a presence in Nepal. Because of the worldliness that accompanies globalization, everyone now has more preconceptions, accurate or not, about everything.

These changes have been felt—in ways that are sometimes subtle and sometimes egregious—in the communities in which all these returned Volunteers now live. Nepal I RPCVs work both sides of the street: they have been globalized by their experiences abroad, and they have been globalizing by their presence in the hundreds of communities in which they have been sprinkled after their return. Many other Americans have returned from similar experiences, in projects sponsored by social service groups and religious missions, but the Peace Corps represents a quantum jump in numbers. As a U.S. government-funded organization, it represents the country in a quasi-official role.

By contrast, most of the comparatively large numbers of those who have served in the armed forces have relatively little cultural experience outside their military bases or off the battlefield. Such social experience for them comes about fitfully and inadvertently. If Peace Corps Volunteers aren't involved culturally in local communities, there is something wrong. For the Peace Corps, achieving such cultural competence is the whole point.

Social

Almost without exception, returned Nepal I Volunteers became known in their communities as local experts on the then still exotic, little-known and mysterious country of Nepal, described in the media (when the media paid any attention at all) mainly by uninformative clichés such as "roof of the world." They were asked to speak to school classes, civic groups, church groups, nursing homes, and community service organizations. Most of the time they illustrated their talks with slides, giving graphic and usually spectacularly colorful representations of the landscape of Nepal and its people, and showing the living conditions they had experienced as Volunteers.

Peter Prindle has almost no connection now with the specific places he worked and visited as a Volunteer, but after his return to the U.S. he renewed his interest in Nepal by earning a Ph.D. in anthropology, with a dissertation on a Brahmin village near the Okhaldunga bazaar in east Nepal. He teaches anthropology at a college in Maine from time to time, and frequently uses Nepalese examples to make his points. If his students had not known about Nepal before, they do after taking one of his courses.

He continues to frequently visit the Brahmin village he studied, and he has financially assisted a number of children in the village to pursue their education, through high school and even, for about a dozen of them, through college. He gets so many requests for help that the situation has gotten out of hand, and he is attempting to establish a foundation to continue this assistance. Thus in the U.S. and in Nepal, Peter continues to quietly remove barriers of social ignorance separating Americans and Nepalis. He is simultaneously a globalized and globalizing presence.

My own experience was similar. I taught anthropology at Carleton College for 38 years, and no matter what the topic of the course was—introductory, theoretical, or more specialized subjects—many of the examples I used in lectures were taken from what I had learned, and was continuing to learn during research sabbaticals, in Nepal. I could tell, from the keen look in their eyes and the way they sat up in their seats, that most of these examples—about caste, diet, religion, politics, and family life (I knew something about family life from the year I lived with a Brahmin family in Kathmandu)—captured their interest more than the humdrum generalities found in text books.

Hal Christianson taught 8th grade social studies in Minnesota and used his slides and artifacts to good effect in the unit on South Asia. It helped make geography more alive, he says, and "sometimes I meet the students that I've had, and they always remember things that I've mentioned about places I've been in Nepal. I think it made it more interesting to them." He also returned to Nepal to teach in the International School there in the 1970s.

Nick Cibrario had a similar experience: "Serving in Nepal changed my life immensely. I had seen things from an American-Catholic perspective. Suddenly you're in a Buddhist/Hindu culture. I was amazed at the knowledge these people had, their history, their background. It just turned my life around. I could never go back to the way I thought before coming to Nepal. The old ways had to be redefined. All my beliefs, I think, had to be examined and redefined.

"I don't think I was conscious of that. It was just a matter of slowly beginning to think, and comparing things. For example, coming home, people were complaining about not having air conditioning. I mean, we were lucky if we

Fig. 16. Ken Martin at bat during a softball game in Tansen.

Fig 17. Jim Fisher riding his bike to work through a back street in Kathmandu.

had electricity or a flush toilet, without worrying about air conditioning. That was the epitome of luxury. Everything had to be thought through a second time, or a third. My life has been changed immensely because of this experience."

Nick entered a Jesuit seminary when he first got back, but left it, in part because his life had become so turned around in Nepal, and taught high school for the rest of his career. "In my classes I mention Nepal constantly, always. Especially in world literature class, devoting time to the Bhagavad Gita, the Mahabharata, the Ramayana—a little bit here and there, the mantras, such as *Om mani padme hum*. I'd speak a little Nepali for them and occasionally bring in someone who had been to India or Nepal. We'd have a little talk-show type of thing. In the regular classes I would often refer to Nepal."

In similar fashion Peter Farquhar felt he was able to pass along what he had learned in Nepal to his students in the community college in California where he taught upon his return: "My slides of Nepal were on the screen, if not daily, almost weekly in my classroom. Yes, many of my students had a good preparation for going out into the world, but you only see certain things when you travel as a tourist. But when you settle down and you live within the culture for an extended period of time, your whole perspective on life changes. Your whole concept of yourself in relationship to the rest of mankind changes. It's a profound thing, exposure to the great religions of Asia—Buddhism and Hinduism. I mean, it does, literally, boggle the mind. But it also provides a tremendous, in a sense, peace ultimately, of feeling at one with the variety of human experience." That feeling is what Peter has tried to transmit to his college geography students in the decades since his return.

Because of her Peace Corps experience, Julie Goetze intervened when a problem developed in the public school her children were attending in Massachusetts. There was a family from Bangladesh who got into great trouble with the school system because the school system didn't understand their culture. A third grade girl was consistently late to school, and she was being taken to court over it. When Julie heard about it, she assigned herself as an advocate for the family, to help straighten things out. She said, "Without my Peace Corps experience, I wouldn't have been brash enough to say, 'This has to be fixed,'" and then to take it upon herself to help fix it. As with the others, Julie was globalized and globalizing at the same time.

Dick Murphy was able to use his experience in Nepal in his high school class on the chemistry of the environment. One of the components of that class was eating. He would ask, "Should you eat meat which is going to require a lot of grain to produce? Or do you focus on the grain and other plants that are grown in the fields?" Then he would talk about that, but it would go a little flat, because students wouldn't realize what he was trying to say. "So then I talked Becky [his wife, also a member of Nepal I] into making some dal [lentils], some rice, and a little bit of fish and greens. We'd serve that up, for all five classes that were meeting on that particular day, so they'd have a little bit of this food. Well, many of the students didn't want to try it, but it did make an impression. I've had students come back and mention that this is one of the things that they remembered."

What these examples show is that returning Volunteers who entered American classrooms brought more than just their college degrees or teaching certificates with them—credentials readily available in the U.S. They also brought a myriad of real life experiences in Nepal that they could transmit to their students, and to the communities they became part of. They obviously enjoyed the opportunity to relive some of those experiences, and apparently these classes were remembered years later by their students. In this way the Volunteers, having been globalized in Nepal, were now globalizing the Americans they got to know after their return, including American students.

Jane Stevens remarked, "After the Peace Corps, you just sort of have the sense of what it's like to be the odd person out in a community, you know, in a positive sort of way. I think after September 11th, Americans are just simply going to have to do a lot of work there. We're basically very kind people and very sharing people, very concerned people, but somehow that's not the image we're giving off

Fig. 18. Students at Pokhara High School explaining the elements on a puja *tray for worshipping Saraswati (Goddess of Learning) to Julie Goetze in Pokhara.*

Fig. 19. Jim Fisher joking with his colleagues at the College of Education in Kathmandu.

in a big part of the world. We've got to do something to turn that around, and the Peace Corps is certainly one way to do that. Any Peace Corps Volunteer who comes home brings with him or her a sense of that caring that just has to have a positive effect. If it doesn't, then we can do nothing, but at least that's one place to start."

Political

For Bob Proctor, life in Nepal fundamentally changed his concept and feelings about the realm of the political, and what is understood by "home." "Home" now had to include Nepal, "and for me 'home' would expand further to include other parts of the world, such as Laos, Lebanon, the Congo, India, and Sri Lanka, because in each of these places where I worked overseas after Nepal, I brought with me a sense of a very elastic and embracing concept of 'home.' A beautiful legacy.

"But it was a legacy not without its dark side. My idiosyncratic sensitivities made it difficult to be elastic and accepting when it came to changes in these various manifestations of home. To me, exploitation from without, and by Nepalis from within, have altered Nepal forever, and for the worse. A horrible war almost ruined the Laos I had embraced with love, and civil war almost did the same thing to 'my' Lebanon. Zaire still remains the epitome of a bloody basket case. And a seemingly endless civil war rages on in my last 'home,' Sri Lanka.

"Perhaps I can be somewhat excused for weeping over what has become of Kathmandu and Nepal—and many of the Nepalese. I witnessed the 'progress' of the changes there, visiting not less than once every two years from 1970 until my last visit in 1988. Yes, I finally had to permit myself to accept that visit as my last. I simply cannot return and feel comfortable anymore, and can only envy those who do. Though I'd give my eye teeth for a chance to spend an hour or two each day in Asan Tole, perhaps partly hidden in the shadow of a shopkeeper's doorframe, in order to take in one of the most fascinating flows of humanity on earth."

"Already, the adult children of my former landlord in Nepal have expressed their profound indebtedness to me for my memoir-style recollections of life with their father, and of life in Kathmandu itself in the early '60s, when they were just little kids. Can one really conceive of a better kind of legacy from me for a country, and a people I love, who have done so much for me?"

The reader might sense a distinctively liberal political stance on the part of most Nepal I Volunteers. Given the Democratic origins of the Peace Corps, it is not surprising that many Volunteers would be inclined that way, to the extent that they were political at all. It's safe to say we were all pro-Kennedy, but not in a hardcore, doctrinaire Democratic way, because the rigid contrast between political parties did not then exist. In the early 1960's there was still some overlap, and good will, between conservative Democrats and liberal Republicans. We regarded conservative critics of the Peace Corps more as old fogies than as political adversaries. We were more pro-Peace Corps than we were pro-Democrats.

Nepal I served in the days of pre-Vietnam innocence, and the America Volunteers had left in 1962 was not the America they returned to in the mid-1960s, full of growing protests against the Vietnam War and continuing demonstrations for civil rights. Popular culture had changed too: the most popular television shows (by Nielsen ratings) in 1961 and 1962 were, respectively, *Wagon Train* and *The Beverly Hillbillies*. By 1971 and 1972 *All in the Family* had taken over the top spot.[44] Technological changes were occurring quickly too: 1962 saw the invention of color Polaroid film, and in 1963 5-digit zip codes were introduced, the Kodak Instamatic camera was developed, and Weight Watchers was founded to help people slim down.[45]

The "bear any burden" rhetoric that gave rise to the Peace Corps also spawned the hubris that America's transformative power knew no limits, resulting in the disaster of the Vietnam War. The innocent idealism of the Kennedy years had given way to the turmoil and rebellion of the Johnson and, later, Nixon years. Volunteers both fought in the Vietnam War (whether drafted or by volunteering because they were going to be drafted) and protested against that war.

The civil rights struggle, which was still in its beginning phases when we went to Nepal, the anti-war movement, which developed after our time there, the environmental[46] and feminist[47] concerns—all these were causes most Nepal I Volunteers came to support almost unthinkingly over the years.[*] The cultural inclinations which moved us to sign up for the Peace Corps in the first place, and which were nurtured by our experiences in Nepal, tended to move us in these directions. Our gut reaction to something that was wrong, or not working, was: what can we do to fix this? Without that attitude we would not have survived two years in Nepal.

There were also several Republicans among our ranks. However, in the same way that many of us were inclined towards the Democrats, but not in an intransigent, dogmatic way, these Republicans were of the progressive, non-ideological sort, perhaps what were called Eisenhower Republicans in the argot of the times—the kind that felt entirely at home in the more generally, but only implicitly, Democratic milieu in which they operated. They would not have been very promising material for today's Tea Party. Al Champney describes himself as originally Republican, and now a socially liberal, fiscally conservative, pessimistic independent. On the other hand, Bill Clayton described himself as originally a Democrat who has now become a Republican, but has never been politically active in either direction.

During the 50th anniversary celebrations in 2011 of the founding of the Peace Corps, even the most conservative, hawkish Republican members of Congress stood up to champion the Peace Corps. The congressional critics from 50

---

[*] Zimmerman (2006: 204) reports that a group of returned PCVs mounted a protest at Peace Corps headquarters in Washington in 1970, stating that "Once abroad, we discovered that we were part of the U.S. worldwide pacification program...to build an Empire for the U.S.... As volunteers we were part of that strategy; we were the Marines in velvet gloves."

years before had not only disappeared—they had vanished
without a trace. All the American Presidents who followed
President Kennedy publicly supported the Peace Corps.
Lyndon Johnson continued his predecessor's personal
interest without missing a beat.[*] Ironically, conservatism as
a political movement had grown much more intense and
focused since those days, but the Peace Corps had become
immune from attack or even criticism from any political
direction. Fifty years after it was founded, the Peace Corps
had become as thoroughly and unarguably American as
Big Macs and apple pie.

Cultural

Several returned Volunteers have commented on the strong
impact Asian religions had on them in Nepal. None converted
in any conventional sense, but many felt they had tapped into
a reservoir of wisdom they had not suspected was there and
could not ignore. Ralph Teague, who pursued South Asian
Studies for a while in graduate school, said: "My studies in
South Asia took me pretty heavily into both Hinduism and
Buddhism, and it did have a strong influence, a very strong
influence in my demeanor, and has been going on over the
past forty years. So that is very much of an influence.

"We have had, I think, way too few people in this country
who have assimilated some of the South Asian culture at
a popular level. Of course, during the sixties, when we all
got back to the U.S., there was a lot of interest in both the
religions, Hinduism and Buddhism, at a popular level, and
some of that has stuck with people, as it has with me. I've had
the opportunity to be in another culture, another religion.
Having had that experience makes you want to adjust your
own reality to the reality that you saw there.[†]

---

[*]   See appendix II for a letter sent by Johnson to King Mahendra in early 1964.

[†]   Like Ralph, I was curious about South Asian religion. I was fortunate
       to meet and interview Shiva Puri Baba, a South Indian *sadhu* living
       in Nepal while we were there. He died a few months after I talked
       to him (his claim to be 136 years old was generally accepted). I very
       much appreciated the sensible and thoughtful answers to the many

"I like the simplicity of the things there. You get by on a lot less than what we have become so accustomed to. Look around and ask yourself, is this a necessary feature in my life? Well, you know, I enjoy my surroundings, living here, having the opportunity to come out here to this summer place on an island in Puget Sound, but it is not the highest thing, the most important thing in my life."

Here, as in so many of these narratives of life after Peace Corps service in Nepal, there is the push to modify a previous, inherited, and unquestioned cultural reality in the light of the attractions of newly discovered actualities. No longer did we assume a metaphysical authority we could export. Instead, we felt a need to adjust our own spiritual sensibilities to powerful other realities we would not have had to confront as tourists, but which as long-term residents we could not ultimately avoid. Nepal was not just different in all the obvious everyday ways; it was an encyclopedia of other cultures that we had to read seriously.

While interests in Asian religion are typically metaphysical, they can also be physical, and even downright medical. Having spent almost five years as a Volunteer, Mac Odell had become quite well versed in the basics of Hinduism (from his time in Dhankuta) and Buddhism (from his time in Sherpa country). As we observed during Peace Corps training, however, Mac was always bursting with enthusiasm and seemed never to run out of energy. It wore as many of us out as it endeared him to others.

For years, however, Mac was unaware that he had all the symptoms of ADD (Attention Deficit Disorder) or, as it's also called, ADHD (Attention Deficit Hyperactivity Disorder), more colloquially known as hyperactivity. A few of us in the group may have recognized the symptoms, but most assumed that this was just the way Mac was wired. Frequently, however, both while he was a Volunteer, and in the following years—until he returned to Nepal in 1994 as Project Manager for The Mountain Institute's Makalu-Barun Conservation Project on the Tibetan border—Mac had wanted to study meditation, a rich heritage of both the

---

questions I posed to him which troubled me at the time.

Fig. 20. Jim Fisher in the process of decapitating a goat to provide the once-a-week meal with meat at Pharping Boarding School.

Fig. 21. Jim Fisher completes the decapitation of the goat.

Hindu and Buddhist faiths. Naturally, with ADD, he never found the time to do so. As Mac tells the story:

"My high energy was getting in the way of both my relationships and my work. My colleagues at The Mountain Institute, however, recognized it for what it was—ADD—and they recommended it be treated. It had never occurred to me that I had ADD; that was something that kids might have that made them bounce off the walls and never be able to concentrate at school. I'd done pretty well in school, however. How could I have ADD?

"Well, at the risk of losing my job, I went for diagnosis and, sure enough, that was me. A regimen of three drugs was prescribed that I had to take five times a day. Being scatter-brained, I had to buy a Timex IronMan watch with five alarms, or I'd forget to take my meds.

"Then I thought about those meditation courses I'd always wanted to take. Of course, I'd always been 'too busy' to take a 10-day meditation course—the highly recommended Vipassana program that originated in India, with the Buddha, made its way to Burma, then back to India and Nepal—Buddha's birthplace—and finally around the world. I signed up, hoping it might help with my ADD. But part of the deal for enrolling required a pledge that included 'No sex, no alcohol, no cigarettes, no drugs…' during the 10-day period. What about my meds? Learning that a dispensation was possible for prescription drugs, I considered asking. But then I thought, 'I've lived for 50 years without those drugs, I can make it through just 10 days.'

"I took the course: 10 days without talking, 10 days just sitting. Could anyone imagine Mac Odell sitting still for 10 days? Especially without talking! But I did it. And actually I found it surprisingly easy. At the end of the course all I had left was my Timex. No more drugs. Meditation did the trick, and it's been doing the trick ever since. I still have ADD, of course, and much of that energy. But at least now I'm not driving my family and friends nuts. I'm able to slow down, smell the roses, even sit waiting in the doctor's office without fidgeting or frantically looking for a magazine. I can drive 10 hours from Washington, DC to Boston without turning on the radio. A spiritual gift from the East. A real gift."

Some of these transcendent realities, while not religious in a formal sense, are spiritual in nature. Joyce Thorkelson reflected that, "Well, if I hadn't done [the Peace Corps], I would have settled down, probably in the central valley of California, and not expanded myself very much. I would have read about things but not done things. With this experience you are never the same again. Nepal is like this big rock that's always been there, like an anchor, you always kind of focus back on it. The memories just keep flashing back at you. They are so clear.

"Once in a while I take out my slides. In my house I have a wooden statue of one of the goddesses. I've got a couple of copper things. Remember the wooden-legged German painter who did ink paintings on rice paper, and he sold them at the Royal Hotel? I bought one of his paintings. Had it rolled up for years and years, and now it's hanging over my fireplace. And so there are things in my house. I have a prayer wheel, and those big pewter anklets dancers wear, I have those on my bookshelf. That is my Nepali shelf. I dust those things and the memories come flooding back.

"Sometimes a smell, an aroma, will trigger memories. I can remember the smell of the guava so much. It was just this heavenly smell. Something like that will just take me right back to Nepal.

"But what is also so interesting is, all these friends we have made, the Peace Corps friends. You have a feeling of comradeship and kinship with them that you just don't have with other people because you have shared this immense experience. Even if you might have been really mad at someone or other at the time over there, or if you didn't particularly like someone, still you have this shared experience. If you walk into a room with them now, you are just close with them." Joyce's memories reflect the inexorable power of globalization—in this case, of being globalized, but also globalizing when, just going through the inexorable processes of living, we go about our daily lives.

Ken Van Sickle said, "I believe the Peace Corps affected

me greatly. I think I have much more appreciation for basic things rather than material goods, the things that people who don't ever leave the U.S. are spoiled with. And being much more tolerant of other people's drawbacks has helped tremendously. I think it's greatly improved my sense of humor, too."

Carl took to heart the cultural differences he observed, and has tried to impart those observations in his classes at the University of California, Davis, where he teaches: "One issue was, if you put something on the desk, but didn't maintain possession of it, someone would take it. But if you maintained possession of it by putting it inside the desk, you could have very valuable things that were never stolen. It got me interested in how cultures have different norms for behaviors. Like, what constitutes stealing. If you judge one culture by your own norms, you can always judge it negatively, you know?

"Another example is that there were forms of nudity that were allowed in America that weren't allowed in Nepal. And forms of nudity allowed in Nepal but not in America—like at that time, women would breast-feed in public, which they wouldn't do in the U.S. [Carl might also have mentioned the erotic statuary carved on temple struts, which would be considered pornographic and therefore banned in the U.S.] So, every culture has the ammunition with which to attack another culture and degrade it. That's something I've used all the time in the classes I teach at my university, with examples from Nepal. I start out with differences in conception of nudity, differences in conception of stealing, in conceptions of cleanliness—how difficult it was for us to wipe our bottoms with water, but how the Nepalis felt that wiping your bottom with toilet paper was just sort of spreading, as they say, sort of spreading the shit around, you know?"

Other Volunteers also kept the embers of globalism glowing by keeping in touch with Nepali friends and counterparts over the years, which gave them an infusion of interest and enthusiasm, even from afar. When Julie attended the Nepal I reunion in Pokhara in 2000, she hadn't been to

Nepal in the 38 years since she had left. "When I arrived at the airport I was actually met by my Nepali counterpart, my physics colleague. I wrote what day I was coming, and he discovered which flight I was on. He was there in his car, with a driver, which of course he didn't have when I knew him. He drove me around Kathmandu, where I didn't recognize anything. It was so full of trucks and cars and stuff. But I thought, "Wow, that was really special to have kept up with him for 38 years. There he was. That was special. So, 38 years of correspondence paid off, and it was wonderful to see him. He was just as energetic as he was then. I could have easily gone and taught more Physics with him. Yeah, great guy." Such vignettes demonstrate the ongoing process of globalization so many ex-Volunteers continue to be part of.

An apt, typical, yet unspectacular example of the way globalizing and being globalized goes on simultaneously, across continents and over generations, is Jerry Young's story of a continuing relationship between his family and that of a Nepalese friend for 50 years. Shortly after he arrived in 1962 in his village, Dhulikhel, just beyond the east end of the Kathmandu Valley, Jerry met a young Nepali who had also arrived in Dhulikhel where he had been assigned as a judge in the district court. Perhaps because they were both young, educated, and outsiders to the village, they struck up a friendship, which was strengthened over the course of long walks together. After two years Jerry's tour of service ended, and Prasad, the judge, was transferred elsewhere, but they stayed in touch.

Prasad eventually got married and took a job with the United Nations, which assigned him to Bangkok. When Jerry was working in Nepal in various jobs over a nine-year period, until 1973, he would always stop in Bangkok to visit with Prasad during his travels back and forth. Years later, in 1999, Jerry returned to Nepal to work in a program of polio eradication, and got in touch with Prasad again, also now back in Nepal. By this time Prasad had two daughters, one living in Canada and one living in the U.S. On one of his trips to visit his daughters, he travelled by way of Wisconsin and spent a week there with Jerry and his family. Then Jerry and his wife went to California while Prasad was visiting his daughter and grandchildren in Los Angeles. Jerry hadn't seen the daughters since they were little girls.

Thus Jerry and Prasad carried on a friendship in Nepal, Thailand, and various parts of the U.S., which has endured for 50 years and continues by email when their paths do not cross. Their relationship has nothing to do with international markets or bank rates. Prasad and Jerry, who had grown up "on a farm in the middle of nowhere in southern Michigan", as he put it, were simply part of a worldwide process of being globalized by each other and globalizing each other. Few, if any, of the thirty or so of us in international fields, like Jerry, would have gone in that direction without the experience in Nepal. Even when we've been promoted to higher administrative positions in the organizations with which we've been involved, the populist orientation is always lurking somewhere in the background, as some of the interview transcripts have shown.

I have portrayed the experiences of Nepal I Volunteers, despite the stresses and strains, both in Nepal and afterwards, ultimately as unalloyed, positive successes. That may overstate the case. I have mentioned two members of the group who left Nepal in 1963 (one was too old to adapt, the other too young). For them, Nepal could not have provided the positive and powerful memories that it did for the rest of us, simply because they were not there long enough to cycle through the ups and downs of the total experience. I did not interview them because I could not find them, but from what they wrote in earlier newsletters I know that they remained much interested in being in touch with their old comrades. I suspect that in retrospect even in their cases, the truncated Nepal experience was like dropping out of college before graduating, in that it provided lasting and affirmative memories for their subsequent lives.

Globalization:
Exemplifications, Excursions, Complications

As a process, globalization can be picked apart and sorted

into various analytical compartments: cultural, political, social, economic, positive, negative, familial, linguistic, religious, and occupational, to name a few. That's what academics tend to do, and, true to form, much of this book follows such a strategy, to impose order on complexity. But any empirical, concrete instance of globalization both displays and conceals all of these features, independent and interdependent as they are, combining them into a seamless whole, simply because that's how life is lived—as a whole, not in fragments. The following story illustrates the ways in which characteristics like these are entwined and tangled in a single episode involving only a few people.

After two years in Nepal, Mac Odell and Barbara Wylie were convinced that reform of the educational system was not only desirable but necessary and, if working conditions were right, possible. Meanwhile, Sherpas in Solu valley, a few days south of the high mountain communities where Hillary was building schools, were building their own schools and needed teachers—and most Nepali teachers had no interest in working in such a remote area. With support from the Minister of Education and influential Sherpa leaders, Mac and Barbara were invited to return for a second tour to open these new schools—a golden opportunity to try out their ideas for changing the culture of education. There, they would work in an elementary school in a Sherpa village, where they could emphasize creativity and critical thinking instead of rote and mindless memorization. This approach was akin to the one Barbara had used in her spare time in the "Happy Free School" she had started in Kathmandu.

Before the Peace Corps came along Barbara had married into a family who, because of her progressive ideas about education and religion (she was much intrigued by Montessori and Theosophy, respectively), thought she was a bit unbalanced. After her divorce she said she was "saved" by the Peace Corps, which considered her not merely sane, but eminently desirable as a Volunteer. During her second tour of service she and Mac lived in the very substantial house of an eminent and politically powerful Sherpa family

in the village of Phaplu in east Nepal. After they got settled
in there they invited Mike Frame, their former housemate in
Dhankuta, now also in his second tour of service at his farm
five days walk to the east, to a mini-reunion of their own.
The occasion was a big Buddhist ceremony, Mani Rimdu, at
Chewang Monastery near Phaplu.

At the end of the first day of the ceremony Mike got a
message that Ang Gyale, a young Sherpa member of the
family, wanted to talk to him. Ang Gyale had had a drink
or two, and knowing that Mike and Mac were friends,
wanted to tell Mike his feelings about Mac and Barbara.
Mike had stumbled, unawares, into the classic love
triangle, being played out in this remote corner of Nepal.
Barbara was beautiful and loved the world and everything
that lived in it, which made her attractive to many men.
But here she was in a tiny village community struggling
with her feelings for Mac and Ang Gyale, for whom she
had developed real affection. In the end she realized she
couldn't have both (the minor irony is that Sherpas practice
polyandry so she could have had both, but that would have
pushed cultural relativism farther than it could go), so she
opted for Ang Gyale. Ang Gyale resented the fact that Mac
and Barbara were living in one room as lovers and felt this
sort of thing would hurt Barbara's reputation. Ang Gyale
explained all this in some detail, and Mike finally got away
by promising to talk to Mac and Barbara and Ang Gyale in
the morning.

But it wasn't just the morning. All the next day was
spent sitting in the balcony at the monastery, drinking salt
tea, eating Tibetan breads, and of course watching the monks
dance in their flamboyant and vibrant costumes. Every
few minutes this routine was interrupted while Mike went
outside for a tete-a-tete with one of the three principals.

Mac developed a plan to leave Barbara and his job in
Phaplu and transfer to the school in Namche Bazaar, where
its head master had previously invited Mac to come teach. It
would take some time to get the transfer officially approved,
and Mac also wanted to say his goodbyes to his students and
friends in Phaplu, so Mike told Ang Gyale Mac needed some

time to make a gracious exit. Ang Gyale wanted Mac gone right away, but he agreed to give Mac some time, provided he separated from Barbara. To Mike it seemed that everything was decided; Mac would leave for Namche Bazaar as soon as possible, and Barbara and Ang Gyale would be free to get married and continue living in Phaplu.

Mike retired that evening, worn out from his diplomatic negotiations and feeling confident that everything would work out. Then sometime after midnight, he and Ang Gyale's older brother were woken up. The older brother went to quiet Ang Gyale, who was in a rage, while Mike went to Mac, who was the object of that rage. The ostensible problem was that Mac had been very keen to see the Sherpas do a rare line dance and, before turning in, had asked Barbara to let him know if this happened so he could come watch it. A while later Barbara and Ang Gyale returned, bubbling about the line dance they'd just taken part in. Mac was upset that Barbara hadn't let him know and gave her a dressing down for not informing him, while Barbara said she hadn't thought it was that important.

Ang Gyale was incensed by all this. His view was that Mac still was holding onto Barbara and all his talk about leaving and endorsing their marriage was baloney. He also felt sure that Mac's anger was a surface sign that Mac had not let go and harbored a grudge against Ang Gyale for taking Barbara away from him. This was the point at which the older brother and Mike were called in to keep the peace.

Mac was really frightened by this turn of events and decided to make a rapid exit—go back to Phaplu, pick up some things, and head to Namche Bazaar in the middle of the night. Mike was sworn to secrecy about this plan. He heard rumors that Ang Gyale had a *khukuri* knife, and also a gun, and was vowing to kill Mac. Mike imagined that all such talk was probably just histrionics resulting from too much drinking. Still, one couldn't be certain.

So Mac slipped away in the moonlight and was packing his gear when he heard Ang Gyale out in front of the house shouting and shooting off his gun, and calling for Mac to come out. Now Mac knew things were really serious and that he was on his own, because everyone who could help was up at the monastery sleeping. With considerable stealth, and inspired by ideas from Hollywood movies, he tied a couple of sheets together, slipped out the back window and was on his way to Namche. Mike figured he must have run most of the way to Namche, because he made it in just a couple of days instead of the normal four.

In the event, Barbara's and Ang Gyale's elegant marriage in Phaplu—the first of a Peace Corps Volunteer to a Nepali—was attended by an assortment of Sherpas, as well as government and Peace Corps officials. Ang Gyale and Barbara adopted two Sherpa children, and in subsequent years they divided their time between California and Nepal, where Barbara taught in the international school in Kathmandu. Tragically, 10 years later, in 1975, she and Ang Gyale, along with Sir Edmund Hillary's wife and younger daughter, were killed in a plane crash after taking off from Kathmandu on a flight to the new mountain airport Hillary had helped build in Phaplu just below a lovely home Ang Gyale and Barbara had built together.

Meanwhile Mac Odell had gone on to help open the new school in Namche Bazaar. Although Namche had had a ramshackle school previously, it rarely had a teacher and students were few, so this was a new school and, as it happened, one that I had helped build the year before as a member of Hillary's Himalayan Schoolhouse Expedition in 1964.

Now about 15 days' trek from Kathmandu—or any road—where letters sent by runner would need a good month for a response, things got even worse. Not just lonely—having lost not one but two good friends in Barbara and Ang Gyale—Mac fell very seriously ill. He was racked with fever, nothing in his Peace Corps medical kit had any effect, and both he and his Sherpa family were sure he was dying. There were no doctors, no radio service, and in those days no cell phones or Internet service. He sweated profusely, tossed and turned, and was racked with pain and hallucinations. He tried to write a farewell letter to his family but was unable to hold a pen.

Then, just as he was sure that the end was near, about 2 a.m. one morning, Mac saw the image of the great Buddhist lama of the area, Trulsik Rinpoche, former abbot of the Rong-buk monastery in Tibet on the other side of Mount Everest. Mac had met the lama, become friends, and admired him greatly. And there he was, appearing as in a dream, vision, or hallucination, hovering over him, offering some kind of prayer. Instantly Mac's fever broke and he felt both con-scious and rejuvenated. He rolled over, tucked his head into his pillow and slept like a baby until dawn. When his fam-ily brought him morning tea, he reported, to their immense delight, that he felt totally recovered.

When Mac finally left Namche after his second tour of duty, he took with him a young Sherpa teacher with whom he had become friends. Kaldhen, the son of a village lama and headman, as a young boy had presented the Sherpa petition requesting schools to Sir Edmund Hillary. That petition eventually resulted in a school in virtually every high mountain village in Sherpa country including, coincidentally, the ones I helped build. Mac and Kaldhen traveled together on a two-month trip to Paris, by foot, train, bus, donkey, bullock cart, oil tanker, and the Orient Express. In Paris Mac successfully passed his GRE exams for graduate school at Cornell, while Kaldhen learned the secrets of the Swiss mountain hospitality business working in a family hotel in Switzerland. Kaldhen continued to the U.S., where he learned more about tourism before returning to Nepal to open the first Nepali-owned trekking company. It was a stunning side-effect of the Peace Corp in Nepal—and yet another example of globalization—that one of Kaldhen's daughters, Kesang, ultimately graduated from Yale on a full scholarship.

So in this convoluted and intricate—some might even say Byzantine—fashion, the globalization of Mac, Barbara, Ang Gyale, Mike, Kaldhen, Sir Edmund Hillary, and me (among other actors, too many to list, waiting in the wings), from our various countries, continents, and islands, jobs, assignments, religions, societies, genders, and age cohorts, worked its way to a more or less constructive and mostly happy conclusion. Globalization was an elemental, requisite part of the whole account, every step of the way. The story embodies it and would be unimaginable without it.

While this entire narrative is a little on the atypical and sensational, not to mention melodramatic, side, probably most of us in Nepal I faced times, events, and circumstances containing some or even all of its components: stress, anxiety, anger, illness, depression, happiness, love, friendship, spirituality, exhilaration, curiosity, and relief—all mixed together with ample portions of fulfillment of one kind or another.

8

CONCLUSION

In September, 2011 the Peace Corps celebrated its 50th birthday with a variety of events as thousands of Returned Peace Corps Volunteers descended on Washington. The Nepalese Ambassador in Washington served delicious Nepalese food at a dinner party for as many former Nepal Volunteers—a few hundred, perhaps—who showed up. He shared his elation at the agreement about to be concluded that would authorize the Peace Corps to return to Nepal in 2012. A few days later both he and Mac Odell spoke at the celebration making all this official. Regardless of how they might be measured, the achievements of Nepal I were enough to lead to some 42 uninterrupted years of Peace Corps accomplishment in Nepal, a record few other countries can match. It is no exaggeration to say that the Peace Corps became as popular in Nepal as it did in America, and as much at the level of average citizens in both countries as among officials in the two governments. However the tale is told, and my version is only one of many possible, the Peace Corps in Nepal was a success story.

Any conclusion to be drawn from all this must address not just the fate of the Volunteers, but the question of what has happened to the Nepalis in these 50 years since we arrived in their country. In parts of this book I have referred to observations Volunteers made about the impact they had, or thought they had, on Nepal and their Nepalese friends. As with the changes in the Volunteers themselves, including their involvement in various stages of the globalization process, many of the changes that have taken place in Nepal would have happened regardless of the presence or absence of the Peace Corps. Changes in education, agriculture, tourism, and politics were inevitable. Nevertheless, the impact of Volunteers on the development of education and agriculture, and on their counterparts and friends, and their mostly happy associations with them, are undeniable.

But that has not necessarily led to a particularly happy situation for many Nepalis. Among other things, "development" has not kept pace with population growth. Due in part to malaria eradication in the Tarai and increased availability of modern health services, resources now have to be shared among over 30 million people, compared to barely 10 million when we arrived in Nepal in 1962. The tremendous strides made by many can be seen in the salutary changes in social indices such as literacy (sharply increased) and poverty (dramatically reduced), but their traditional world no longer carries the heft it once did, while many of the benefits of the modern world are still beyond their reach. This has led to many Nepalis, like many people elsewhere in the world, being "caught between two worlds—one a 'cultural' world, only partially intact, wholly diminished, with scant resources for creating a future— the other, 'modern and globalized,' from which they are simultaneously excluded, exploited, and seduced."[48]

Nepalis are caught between those two worlds, among others: a political world sharply fractured by 10 years of a fierce Maoist insurgency; rural areas now partially penetrated by urban markets; cities such as Kathmandu paralyzed by traffic, saturated with pollution, and bloated with a huge population. These worlds are now more connected than ever—cell phone towers dot the remotest hills and valleys. But everywhere, people who are increasingly literate have few employable skills or prospects for jobs, other than what can be found in the Middle East (by over a million migrant Nepali workers), or in India (by more than two million migrant Nepalis). These are all partially globalized people with little chance of receiving any of the benefits which accrue to the class of highly educated, comfortable, mostly high-caste urban dwellers who are world travelers and who monopolize the political and economic resources available to the country. Globalization has losers as well as winners. Not for nothing did most of the rural population rise up in revolt against their King, his army, and the more privileged classes of the country. The story of those who globalization has left behind is a bittersweet tale that is yet to be told.

Taking the story in the direction of what we do know more about, what can we conclude, from their narratives, about the experience of Volunteers in the first Peace Corps group to Nepal—remembered now by its members somewhat unrealistically as a heroic saga? From the point of view of most members of that group, it has become larger than life. As the decades have passed, the stories have become more fanciful, but occasional meetings (and being interrogated for this book) serve as a reality check on runaway, vivid imaginations.

What we did is not necessarily what we thought we were doing at the time. Our earnest desire to do good—i.e., to *accomplish* good—could be equally and ultimately seen as arrogance and doomed to fail, and some of us seem to have concluded something like that. We thought we were going to save the world, but most of us came to the gradual realization that we were only, or at least mainly, saving ourselves. We thought we had answers to other people's problems, but we came away with more answers to our own problems. Whether the Peace Corps helped the world or not, it did change many American lives profoundly, and that was, and continues to be, a good thing. About Nepal's problems we came away puzzled, with more questions than answers. We went to Nepal as children, and returned as adults.

The Peace Corps experience propelled many of us into international fields. Very few would have pursued such careers without the Nepal years under our belts. Are we therefore pawns of the American military-industrial-diplomatic complex? No, because even in our pre-Vietnam artlessness that same Peace Corps experience gave us a grassroots orientation which is subversive of the modus operandi of the traditional major actors in that complex. Even when we've been posted abroad in such establishment organizations as the U.S. Foreign Service, USAID, USIS, U.N. agencies, corporations, and private foundations, not to mention the armed forces, a part of us in those assignments has felt the tug of the rank and file connections we recognize need to be part of any successful international program of change. Even when we get kicked upstairs and sit in offices, we cannot escape the knowledge that there's a very different world outside, which we ignore at our peril.

The Peace Corps both globalized us in Nepal and transformed us into globalizing agents at home—it turned us into double agents. Those of us in international work continued to add to our professional skills, bringing more knowledge back to Nepal again in some cases, at higher professional levels. In this way, Peace Corps ideals, spirit, and lessons became embedded in the institutions Nepal continued to develop, such as national parks, health programs, tourism, and universities.

It's true that many of us continued our educations after Peace Corps, but who is to say that we wouldn't have done so anyway? The interviews show that with almost no exceptions we all pursued higher degrees, and many have confessed that they wouldn't have done so without the impetus of what we discovered about ourselves, and the world, while in Nepal. And even if we had returned to the academy without that liberating experience, we would have returned to study different subjects than the ones we did pursue because we went to Nepal.

It is also true that many of us pursued fields and jobs we wouldn't have considered before. Vocations shifted, and continued to shift as we have moved from job to job and pursued new interests and opportunities. Occupational movement, which was invariably upward, also meant class movement. We may have all been originally middle-class, but now we occupy higher echelons in that amorphous group. The rising economic tide in the decades following our time in Nepal did not raise all boats in Nepal, but it certainly raised ours.

One characteristic of our group, over the 50 years since we left Nepal, is its occupational ordinariness. The jobs and positions we've gone on to fill are all straight out of the American vocational mainstream: teacher, farmer, mechanic, town planner, prison guard, banker, bureaucrat, corporate employee, writer, architect, international development consultant. We produced no Senators or Cabinet members, no multi-millionaires, no corporate CEOs, not even any doctors, and only one lawyer. Even in the organizations that employ us we are the ultimate non-organization people. But—and this is the significant part for assessing our impact—we are everywhere. That returned PCVs comprise 30% of USAID and Department of State staffing today is only one example of this.

Our group produced 14 Ph.D.'s. Although most members of Nepal I are authors in the sense that we have produced myriad in-house reports, assessments, analyses, and evaluations for the organizations that have employed us, no fewer than 10 (some Ph.D.'s, some not) have written "real books"—i.e., produced and published for the public market by mainstream publishers. Some of these books are about Nepal, but most are not.

We all came back with a greatly expanded and nuanced sense of cultural relativity and tolerance for different ways of life. None of us converted to an Asian religion, but almost all of us came away with an enhanced appreciation of what those religions have to offer the people who practice them as well as ourselves. Some have spent the rest of their lives studying these other ways of life. A few found that they could not go home again and returned to Nepal to live that other way of life for the rest of their days.

Those who settled in the U.S.—and that's most of us—have been affected in many dimensions of our lives, such as our view of international relations and the wisdom of U.S. governmental and military intervention. The civil war in Nepal (1996-2006) was cruel and vicious, but it was ultimately settled peacefully—by Nepalis, not by foreign agencies, embassies, or armies. In the event of American intervention (highly unlikely in a country with no tempting geopolitical or economic assets), the members of Nepal I (and later groups) would have largely stood shoulder to shoulder with ordinary Nepalis in raising their voices against such adventuristic meddling.

Our time in Nepal, when we all unwittingly became

globalized, also affected the communities in which we live in this country and which we have been globalizing ever since. We didn't do this singlehandedly. The communities in which we've been living were changing anyway, and we were just one of many factors contributing to the globalization of these communities—the Vietnam War, the civil rights movement, the rise of multiculturalism, immigration, de-industrialization and outsourcing, and tourism—all these played a part, but we were players too. We were supposed to be agents of change in Nepal, but we ended up being agents of change in our own country as well as in Nepal—probably more so, since as insiders we already knew the language and culture.

President Kennedy's innovative administrative initiative produced a cadre of citizens enormously interested and invested in the rest of the world, in ways not possible before the Peace Corps came along. The experience of our group in Nepal is only one miniscule example of that. Now, some 200,000 strong, and having come back from 139 countries, we RPCVs are legion.

There is a fundamental and inescapable truth underlying the ripple effect of RPCVs in this country. Wherever we are we exert a globalizing presence that would be absent without us. One by one each person's effect is small, but our numbers and pervasiveness make us insidiously effective. Corporate and big-country globalism has to take Returned Peace Corps Volunteers (not to mention the thousands who have served in organizations similar to Peace Corps and inspired by it) into account. The second and third goals of the Peace Corps (those concerned with mutual understanding) have been accomplished in ways its founders could have scarcely imagined, and would have sometimes balked at.

Most importantly, we have shared that international interest with the communities we became part of during the following decades—not so much because we were evangelical, but because we were, simply and naturally and unintentionally, what we had become. As agents of change we have been sometimes quiet and sometimes noisy (more than one of us has been arrested at an anti-Vietnam protest), in an expanding and increasingly internationalized and globalized United States. Our presence wherever we've ended up over the past 50 years, and that of the almost 4,000 other Peace Corps Volunteers who followed us to Nepal, has inexorably moved the United States to a more expanded, knowledgeable, proactive, and, especially, tolerant and sympathetic view of that part of the world. To calculate our multiplier effect, add to our experience that of hundreds of thousands of Volunteers in another 138 countries, and the impacts become inescapably palpable.

We are part of a dialectical process of being globalized and globalizing which has acquired a rhythm, voice, and momentum of its own. The Peace Corps is now so deeply engrained in the national consciousness that even though it is of relatively recent vintage in the context of U.S. history, like the Golden Gate Bridge or the Empire State Building, it is hard to imagine now a time without its iconic presence.

When the Peace Corps was founded 50 years ago, it seemed like a radically new step for the United States to take. To some it was naïve and ill-conceived; to others it was hopeful and buoyant. Its critics regarded it as an idealistic project that would founder on the shoals of innocence. They thought it was destined to failure because we Americans knew so little about all the remote and obscure places we were going to go. It is true that we knew little—almost nothing in the case of Nepal—about where we were going to go. What the critics failed to imagine was that we would take the trouble to find out.

The New Frontier temperament had a different take on where we needed to go in the 1960s. According to this outlook, if we were willing to "bear any burden, meet any hardship," we could do anything or go anywhere, whether the destination was a distant, godforsaken, unheard of place like Nepal, or a distant, godforsaken place everyone on earth knows about—the moon. For some, especially those who knew little about Nepal or the moon, those places were equally remote, removed from everyday American life, irrelevant to it, and a waste of time and money to pursue. For others, going to these places posed challenges, however disparate, to be met. As it happened, and against the odds, in the same decade we went to both Nepal and the moon. But they were opposites in more than a celestial sense. Everyone knew about the moon, but almost no earthling went there, while very few knew about Nepal, and thousands went there.

Eventually, for what was at bottom perhaps the same reason—a failure of nerve—we also eventually abandoned both Nepal and the moon. The jury is still out on the moon, but the Peace Corps returned to Nepal in 2012 to take up where it had left off in 2004. It was able to do so because the pioneering spirit of Nepal I had been carried forward, diligently and indefatigably, by 193 other groups of Peace Corps Volunteers assigned to that country over 42 years.

Now, having been planted and nurtured in 139 countries on all continents and grown to maturity in the seed beds from which it sprang, the Peace Corps has become, fifty years after it was founded, a signature and indelible piece of a relentlessly globalized and globalizing America, and the world of which it is inextricably a part.

Now, thousands upon thousands of Nepalis come to the U.S. every year for education, business, pleasure, or to visit family members who live in the U.S. permanently, some of them U.S. citizens. Thousands upon thousands of Americans go to Nepal every year to see the exquisite architecture, trek in the mountains, try the food, search for religious truths, study, or, like Peace Corps Volunteers, just to see old friends. It has all become a natural, routine, and unremarkable process of ubiquitous, inexorable, globalizing exchange, so much so that we scarcely notice we're doing it.

APPENDIX I

Nepal I Peace Corps Volunteers:
Their Ages and Origins

Al Adkins, 18	Lake Stevens, Washington
Paul Ahrens, 28	Hicksville, New York
Elbie Baughman, 25	Blue Mound, Illinois
Doug Bingham, 22	Colchester, Connecticut
Bill Carter, 20	Conway, New Hampshire
Helen Carter, 23	San Diego, California
Al Champney, 23	Romulus, Michigan
Hal Christensen, 22	Harmony, Minnesota
Nick Cibrario, 21	Kenosha, Wisconsin
Bill Clayton, 21	Belton, South Carolina
Larry Dornacker, 21	Blair, Nebraska
Bob Drake, 22	Santa Monica, California
Ron Elliott, 23	Hillsboro, New Hampshire
Rich Emde, 19	St. Louis, Missouri
Peter Farquhar, 24	Berkeley, California
Jim Fisher, 22	Ashland, Kentucky
Beverly Fogg, 21	Hancock, New Hampshire
Mike Frame, 21	Northfield, Minnesota
Les Gile, 21	Rochester, New Hampshire
Julie Goetze, 25	Cambridge, Massachusetts
Rolf Goetze, 24	Cambridge, Massachusetts
Peter Grote, 23	Rangely, Maine
Ralph Hambrick, 21	Sarasota, Florida
Flemming Heegaard, 25	Menlo Park, California
Sam Hunt, 20	Granville, Iowa
Peter Johnson, 21	Coleraine, Minnesota
Carl Jorgensen, 21	Washington, D.C.
Dorothy Kinder, 24	San Bernardino, California
Mel Kinder, 24	San Bernardino, California
David Kollasch, 25	Bancroft, Iowa
Ron Kreeger, 26	Camp Douglas, Wisconsin
Joann Marchand, 21	Canon City, Colorado
Ken Martin, 22	Tampico, Illinois

Don McCleary, 22 — Houston, Texas
Dorothy Mierow, 42 — Colorado Springs, Colorado
Lulu Miller, 61 — Washington, D.C.
Becky Murphy, 20 — Weirs, New Hampshire
Bob Murphy, 29 — Spring Valley, Wisconsin
Dennis Murphy, 23 — Yakima, Washington
Dick Murphy, 22 — Weirs, New Hampshire
Richard Nishihara, 18 — Makawao, Hawaii
Mac Odell, 23 — Shirley Center, Massachusetts
George Peck, 22 — Colorado Springs, Colorado
Dan Pierce, 21 — Balboa, California
Peter Prindle, 23 — Sherborn, Massachusetts
Bob Proctor, 25 — Santa Fe, New Mexico
Bert Puchtler, 25 — Vestal, New York
Bob Rhoades, 20 — Duncan, Oklahoma
Les Richardson, 49 — Mt. Pleasant, Texas
Suki Saltonstall, 26 — North Andover, Massachusetts
Gary Schaller, 22 — Maynard, Minnesota
Mark Schroeder, 25 — Belvidere, Vermont
Franqui Scott, 22 — Red Bluff, California
Jim Scott, 22 — Red Bluff, California
Dave Sears, 21 — West Plains, Missouri
Bob Shrader, 19 — Harrisville, West Virginia
Mimi Smith, 22 — Alexandria, Virginia
Berny Snoeyer, 22 — Grand Rapids, Michigan
Jane Stevens, 19 — Canton, Illinois
Ralph Teague, 23 — College Place, Washington
Joyce Thorkelson, 21 — Patterson, California
Dave Towle, 21 — Concord, New Hampshire
Lee Tuveson, 23 — Downers Grove, Illinois
Ken Vansickle, 19 — Ellendale, North Dakota
Mickey Veich, 25 — Whittier, California
Glenda Warren, 22 — Fort Bliss, Texas
John White, 19 — Frierson, Louisiana
Larry Wolfe, 25 — Garrison, Kentucky
Barbara Wylie, 33 — Ypsilanti, Michigan
Jerry Young, 23 — Reading, Michigan

APPENDIX II

President Johnson wrote the following letter* to King Mahendra barely six weeks after the assassination of President Kennedy.

January 2, 1964

Your Majesty:

My good friend, Sargent Shriver, brings you my very warm personal greetings. I have asked him to reaffirm our full support to Nepal as it seeks to maintain its independence and develop in a way of its own choosing.

I have also asked him to convey to you our deep appreciation for your warm welcome to the 101 Peace Corps Volunteers in your country. Since its birth under President Kennedy, I have regarded the Peace Corps as one of the most imaginative instruments ever devised for capturing the idealism of youth and putting it to work in the cause of world peace and understanding.

Our Volunteers have benefitted enormously from their experience in your country. The United States will also benefit as they return, with broader horizons and greater understanding of the world, to take their places in our society. They will add a new dimension to American life. I only hope that, while with you, they have contributed to the well-being of your people and to their understanding of us.

Although I haven't had the opportunity of visiting Nepal, I have long been interested in your efforts to improve the lot of your people. Mr. Shriver will bring me back a first-hand account of the good progress you have made.

Sincerely,
(signed Lyndon B. Johnson)

His Majesty
Mahendra Bir Bikram Shah Deva
King of Nepal

---

*   Source: LBJ Library, Correspondence File 'NEPAL December 1963-March 1966'.

ENDNOTES

CHAPTER ONE

1 For more on the view of the 1950s as an age of relaxed, complacent people, see Patterson, *Grand Expectations.*

2 For my research on northwest Nepal, northeast Nepal, and the high Hindu castes in Kathmandu, see, respectively, my works *Trans-Himalayan Traders; Sherpas;* and *Living Martyrs.*

3 Levitt, Theodore, "Globalization of Markets."

4 Steger, *Globalization,* 15.

5 Zeiler, "Globalization," 135.

6 For more on world-systems theory, see Wallerstein, *Modern World System.*

7 Steger, *Globalization,* 2.

8 Tsing, *Friction,* 71.

9 Giddens, *Runaway World,* 30.

10 See Ho, "Situating Global Capitalisms," 138.

11 For more on the McDonaldization of the world, see Watson, ed., *Golden Arches East.*

12 Inda and Rosaldo, "Tracking Global Flows," 25.

13 Lodge, *Case for the Generalist.*

14 For more on the notion of cultures as separate and autonomous entities, see Wolf, *Europe and the People Without History.*

15 See Appadurai, *Modernity at Large.*

16 For more on the view from tertiary, peripheral regions, see Taussig, *Devil and Commodity Fetishism.*

17 The stanzas are from "Little Gidding" in *Four Quartets.*

18 The phrase originated in the Sermon on the Mount, and was popularized in a sermon written by Puritan John Winthrop in 1630.

19 See Said, *Orientalism.*

20 For more on this question, see Hoffman, *All You Need Is Love.*

21 See, for example, Messerschmidt, *Anthropologists at Home*; Trencher, *Mirrored Images*; and Ortner, *New Jersey Dreaming*.

22 For more on multi-sitedness, see Hannerz, *Transnational Connections*.

23 For more on the Peace Corps as a new kind of colonialism, see Asad, ed., *Anthropology and the Colonial Encounter*.

24 See Anderson, *Imagined Communities*.

25 See, for example, Ashabrenner, *Moment in History*; Redmon, *Come as You Are*; and Searles, *Peace Corps Experience*.

26 Eckes and Zeiler, *Globalization and the American Century*, 158.

27 For more on transnational flows, see Appadurai, "Disjuncture and Difference."

28 Tsing, *Friction*, 272.

29 For more on the question of the usefulness of the insider/outsider dichotomy, see Narayan, "How Native Is a 'Native' Anthropologist?"

CHAPTER TWO

30 For more on the negative image of the Ugly American, see Lederer and Burdick, *The Ugly American*.

CHAPTER THREE

31 See Latham, *Modernization as Ideology*.

32 For more on creating a romance of peace equal to that of war, see Kessler, *Journey to the Abyss*.

33 Farber and Bailey, *Columbia Guide*, 352.

34 Frame, *Stone House in Pokhara*, 221–222.

35 Farber and Bailey, *Columbia Guide*, 337.

36 For more on the taboo against discussing class background, see Ortner, *New Jersey Dreaming*.

37 For more on Bob Bates, see Bates, *Love of Mountains*.

38 For more on Willi Unsoeld, see Leamer, *Ascent*.

39 Outward Bound's slogan was adopted from Tennyson's original: "To strive, to seek, to find, and not to yield."

CHAPTER FOUR

40   For more on the attitudes of these earlier teachers, see Zimmerman, *Innocents Abroad.*

CHAPTER SEVEN

41   Frame, *Stone House in Pokhara,* 139.
42   Ibid., 185.
43   Some of the details of these experiences are contained in my *Sherpas.*
44   Farber and Bailey, *Columbia Guide,* 401–402.
45   Ibid., 445.
46   Rachel Carson's *Silent Spring* was published in 1962 (Farber and Bailey, *Columbia Guide,* 438).
47   Betty Friedan's *The Feminine Mystique* was published in 1963 (Farber and Bailey, *Columbia Guide,* 439).
48   Green, Linda. "Mayan Youth and Rural Industrialization."

BIBLIOGRAPHY

Anderson, Benedict. *Imagined Communities: Reflections on the Origin and Spread of Nationalism*. London: Verso, 1983.

Appadurai, Arjun. "Disjuncture and Difference in the Global Cultural Economy." *Public Culture* (2) 2: 1–24, 1990.

----------------. *Modernity at Large: Cultural Dimensions of Globalization*. Minneapolis: University of Minnesota Press, 1996.

Asad, Talal, ed. *Anthropology and the Colonial Encounter*. New York: Humanities Press, 1973.

Ashabrenner, Brent K. *A Moment in History: The First Ten Years of the Peace Corps*. Garden City, N.Y.: Doubleday, 1971.

Bates, Robert H. *The Love of Mountains is Best: Climbs and Travels from K-2 to Kathmandu*. Peter Randall, 1994.

Dooley, Tomas. *The Night They Burned the Mountain*. New York: Farrar, Straus and Cudahy, 1956.

Eckes, Alfred E. and Thomas W. Zeiler. *Globalization and the American Century*. Cambridge: Cambridge University Press, 2003.

Eliot, T. S. *Four Quartets*. New York: Harcourt, 1943.

Farber, David and Beth Bailey. *The Columbia Guide to America in the 1960s*. New York: Columbia University Press, 2001.

Fischer, Louis. *The Life of Mahatma Gandhi*. New York: Harper and Brothers, 1950.

Fisher, James. F. *Trans-Himalayan Traders: Economy, Society, and Culture in Northwest Nepal*. Berkeley: University of California Press, 1986.

----------. *Sherpas: Reflections on Change in Himalayan Nepal*. Foreword by Sir Edmund Hillary. Berkeley: University of California Press, 1990.

----------. *Living Martyrs*. Delhi: Oxford University Press, 1997.

Frame, Mike. *A Stone House in Pokhara, and Other Tales*. Northfield, Minnesota: Larchill Press, 2011.

Giddens, Anthony. *Runaway World: How Globalization Is Reshaping Our Lives*. London: Routledge, 2000.

Green, Linda. "Notes on Mayan Youth and Rural Industrialization in Guatemala." *The Anthropology of Globalization*: 101-120. Oxford: Blackwell Publishing, 2008.

Hagen, Toni. *Nepal*. Berne: Kummerly & Fry, 1961.

Hannerz, Ulf. *Transnational Connections*. New York: Routledge, 1996.

Hilton, James. *Lost Horizon*. New York: William Morrow, 1934.

Ho, Karen. "Situating Global Capitalisms: A View from Wall Street." *The Anthropology of Globalization*: 137–164. Oxford: Blackwell Publishing, 2008.

Hoffman, Elizabeth Cobbs. *All You Need Is Love: The Peace Corps and the Spirit of the 1960s*. Cambridge: Harvard University Press, 1998.

Inda, Jonathan Xavier and Renato Rosaldo. "Tracking Global Flows." *The Anthropology of Globalization*: 3–46. Oxford: Blackwell Publishing, 2008.

Kessler, Count Harry. *Journey to the Abyss: The Diaries of Count Harry Kessler, 1880-1918*. New York: Knopf, 2011.

Latham, Michael E. *Modernization as Ideology: American Social Science and "Nation Building" in the Kennedy Era.* Chapel Hill: University of North Carolina Press, 2000.

Leamer, Laurence. *Ascent: The Spiritual and Physical Quest of Willi Unsoeld.* New York: Simon and Schuster, 1982.

Lederer, William J., and Eugene Burdick. *The Ugly American.* New York: Norton, 1958.

Levitt, Theodore. "The Globalization of Markets." *Harvard Business Review*, May–June 1983.

Lodge, George C. *The Case for the Generalist in Rural Development.* Washington, D.C.: Peace Corps Office of Public Affairs, 1969.

Messerschmidt, Donald A. *Anthropologists at Home in North America: Methods and Issues in the Study of One's Own Society.* New York: Cambridge University Press, 1981.

Morris, Harold, and E. Robert Hellawell. *Completion of Service Conference.* Washington, D.C.: Peace Corps, 1964.

Narayan, Kirin. "How Native Is a 'Native' Anthropologist?" *American Anthropologist* 95: 671–86.

Ochs, Elinor, and Lisa Capps. "Narrating the Self." *Annual Review of Anthropology* 25: 19–43.

Ortner, Sherry B. *New Jersey Dreaming: Capital, Culture, and the Class of '58.* Durham, NC: Duke University Press, 2003.

Patterson, James T. *Grand Expectations: The United States, 1945-1974.* Oxford: Oxford University Press, 1997.

Pieterse, Jan Nederveen. *Globalization and Culture.* Lanham, MD: Rowman and Littlefield, 2009.

Redmon, Coates. *Come as You Are: The Peace Corps Story.* San Diego: Harcourt Brace Jovanovich, 1986.

Said, Edward W. *Orientalism.* New York: Vintage Books, 1994.

Searles, P. David. *The Peace Corps Experience: Challenge and Change, 1969-1976*. Lexington, KY: University Press of Kentucky, 1997.

Schweitzer, Albert. *Out of My Life and Thought*. New York: Henry Holt and Company, 1931.

Steger, Manfred B. *Globalization: A Very Short Introduction*. Oxford, Oxford University Press, 2009.

Taussig, Michael T. *The Devil and Commodity Fetishism in South America*. Chapel Hill: University of North Carolina Press, 1984.

Tsing, Anna Lowenhaupt. "The Global Situation." *The Anthropology of Globalization*: 66–98. Oxford: Blackwell Publishing, 2008.

------------. *Friction: An Ethnography of Global Connection*. Princeton, NJ: Princeton University Press, 2005.

Trencher, Susan R. *Mirrored Images: American Anthropology and American Culture, 1960–1980*. Westport, CT: Bergin and Garvey, 2000.

Wallerstein, Immanuel. *The Modern World System: Capitalist Agriculture and the Origins of the European World-Economy in the 16th Century*. New York: Academic Press, 1974.

Watson, James, ed. *Golden Arches East: McDonald's in East Asia*. Palo Alto: Stanford University Press, 2006.

Wolf, Eric. *Europe and the People Without History*. Los Angeles: University of California Press, 1982.

Zeiler, Thomas W. "Globalization." *Encyclopedia of American Foreign Policy*. New York: Charles Scribner's Sons, 2002.

Zimmerman, Jonathan. *Innocents Abroad, American Teachers in the American Century*. Cambridge, MA: Harvard University Press, 2006.

INDEX

The purpose of BIBLIOTHECA HIMALAYICA is to make available works on the natural history and civilizations of Central Asia and the Himalaya. The selection of books includes new works by present-day scholars and students, as well as reprints of classical, out-of-print or antiquarian books. Reprints of older books may include additional contemporary illustrations as well as an up-to-date introduction.

BIBLIOTHECA HIMALAYICA was founded by H. K. Kuløy in 1969. There are four series in Bibliotheca Himalayica.
SERIES I: History – Geography – Travel
SERIES II: Linguistics – Bibliography – Biography – Literature
SERIES III: Art – Archaeology – Architecture – Religion – Ethnology
SERIES IV: Ecology – Environment – Development Studies

SERIES I: HISTORY – GEOGRAPHY – TRAVEL

Vol. 1 JOURNEY TO LHASA AND CENTRAL TIBET, Sarat Chandra Das (1909), 1970.

Vol. 2 REPORT ON A VISIT TO SIKHIM AND THE THIBETAN FRONTIER, John Ware Edgar (1874), 1969.

Vol. 3 AN ACCOUNT OF THE KINGDOM OF NEPAUL, Colonel Kirkpatrick (1811), 1969.

Vol. 4 AN ACCOUNT OF AN EMBASSY TO TIBET, Samuel Turner (1800), 1971.

Vol. 5 BHOTAN AND THE STORY OF THE DOOAR WAR, David Field Rennie (1866), 1970.

Vol. 6 NARRATIVES OF THE MISSION OF GEORGE BOGLE TO TIBET, AND THE JOURNEY OF THOMAS MANNING TO LHASA, Clements Markham (1876), 1971.

Vol. 7 POLITICAL MISSIONS TO BOOTAN, Ashley Eden (1865), 1972.

Vol. 8 GAZETTEER OF SIKHIM (1894), 1972.

Vol. 9 (not used)

Vol. 10 AN ACCOUNT OF THE KINGDOM OF NEPAL, Francis Buchanan Hamilton (1819), 1971.

Vol. 11 WESTERN HIMALAYAS AND TIBET, Thomas Thomson (1852), 1979.

Vol. 12 THE ABODE OF SNOW, Andrew Wilson (1875), 1979.

Vol. 13 A NORWEGIAN TRAVELLER IN TIBET, Per Kvaerne 1973.

Vol. 14 A STUDY IN NEPALI ECONOMIC HISTORY, Mahesh Chandra Regmi 1972, 1978.

Vol. 15 THE RISE OF THE HOUSE OF GORKHA, L. F. Stiller S. J. 1973.

Vol. 16 SIKKIM, Colman Macaulay (1885), 1977.

SERIES II: LINGUISTICS – BIBLIOGRAPHY – BIOGRAPHY – LITERATURE

CPSIA information can be obtained at www.ICGtesting.com
Printed in the USA
BVOW040123140613

323299BV00001B/4/P